Family Circle | **breads and sweet rolls cookbook**

Family Circle®

BREAD and SWEET ROLLS
COOKBOOK

FAMILY CIRCLE LIBRARY OF CREATIVE COOKING

**A Practical Guide to creative cooking containing special material from Family Circle
Magazine and the Family Circle Illustrated Library of Cooking**

ROCKVILLE HOUSE PUBLISHERS
GARDEN CITY, NEW YORK 11530

on the cover:
A smashing array of breads, fit for any table: **Old Milwaukee Rye Bread, One Hundred Percent Whole Wheat Bread, Corn Bubble Bread,** and two shaped yeast breads.

on the back cover:
Baking is creating and what could be more creative than the **Perfect Corn Muffins** (top) and the wide assortment of yeast and quick breads (below).

opposite title page:
Easy, fast-to-make basic Danish Pastry Dough is used for a variety of pastries such as **Cheese Danish.**

Publishing Staff

Editor: MALCOLM E. ROBINSON
Design and Layout: MARGOT L. WOLF
Production Editor: DONALD D. WOLF

For Family Circle

Editorial Director: ARTHUR M. HETTICH
Editor Family Circle Books: MARIE T. WALSH
Assistant Editor: CERI E. HADDA

A QUICK METRIC TABLE FOR COOKS

Liquid Measures

1 liter	4¼ cups (1 quart + ¼ cup *or* 34 fluid ounces)	1 gallon	3.785 liters
1 demiliter (½ liter)	2⅛ cups (1 pint + ⅛ cups *or* 17 fluid ounces)	1 quart	0.946 liter
1 deciliter (1/10 liter)	A scant ½ cup *or* 3.4 fluid ounces	1 pint	0.473 liter
1 centiliter (1/100 liter)	Approximately 2 teaspoons *or* .34 fluid ounce	1 cup	0.237 liter *or* 237 milliliters
1 milliliter (1/1000 liter)	Approximately 1/5 teaspoon *or* .034 fluid ounce	1 tbsp.	Approximately 1.5 centiliters *or* 15 milliliters

Weights

1 kilogram	2.205 pounds	1 pound	0.454 kilogram *or* 453.6 grams
500 grams	1.103 pounds *or* about 17.5 ounces	½ pound	0.226 kilogram *or* 226.8 grams
100 grams	3.5 ounces	¼ pound	0.113 kilogram *or* 113.4 grams
10 grams	.35 ounce	1 ounce	28.35 grams
1 gram	0.035 ounce		

Linear Measures

1 meter	1.09 yards *or* 3.28 feet *or* 39.37 inches	1 yard	0.914 meter
1 decimeter (1/10 meter)	3.93 inches	1 foot	0.3048 meter *or* 3.048 decimeters *or* 30.48 centimeters
1 centimeter (1/100 meter)	0.39 inch	1 inch	2.54 centimeters *or* 25.4 millimeters
1 millimeter (1/1000 meter)	0.039 inch		

Contents

All it takes is one basic Danish Pastry dough. With it you can cook a variety of eye-catching and taste-tempting Danish, especially this **Mayor's Braid.**

Introduction

DO YOU REMEMBER watching your grandmother kneading the dough, carefully sprinkling flour on the large mound of glutinous material? And later, smelling the newly-baked bread long before it was taken out, golden-brown from the oven.

There were loaves, and muffins, brightly colored fruit breads, and pans-full of poppy seed rolls.

Or do you recall munching into your favorite Danish, the springy bread still hot; or smothering a stack of pancakes with butter and maple syrup?

If you do, you understand a little of the joy and satisfaction of baking bread. And can understand why there is a great increase in people who are doing their own thing in the kitchen.

And this is what the **Breads and Sweet Rolls Cookbook** is all about—giving you a wide selection of quick and yeast bread recipes to choose from.

Yeast breads are treated first. There are yeast breads that are made with flour and yeast, and those which use a sourdough starter. If you've never tried baking from a batch of sourdough, you're in for a surprise. There is an old legend that sourdough was brought across the Atlantic with the Pilgrims. While we know that this is not possible—the dough would have spoiled—it still bears out the importance of sourdough to those early bread cooks. Borrow a starter from a friend. Then watch as other people borrow from you.

Quick breads are the other main type of bread. They do not rely on yeast for the raising, but instead are made with an all-purpose flour. There are coffee cakes, waffles, breads, doughnuts, dumplings, and a wide assortment of muffins and biscuits. And because of the availability of convenience foods, which are quick breads, there is a section especially devoted to cooking your favorite breads with these hurry-up ingredients.

Do-It-Yourself Yeast Breads

For anyone who wants to get back to basics, cooking breads from a dough that has been kneaded by hand is totally satisfying. And the results are fruit, nut, and cheese breads, gluten breads, and a host of other delectable made-from-scratch breads that you, your family and friends can enjoy straight from the oven.

ALL-OCCASION BREADS

Sourdough Bread

Since the days of the gold rush in Alaska, people have been making a special type of bread that uses the yeast in the air as the leavening agent. The bread is called sourdough because of the particular flavor that the starter gives to the bread. Our method takes about 7 days to make, but once you have your starter made, measure the required amount for the recipe and replace with an equal amount of flour and milk. In the past, people had more time, so only the sourdough starter was used to raise the bread—it took 24 hours. To quicken the process we add commercial yeast, but you will still get that special flavor.

Bake at 400° for 40 minutes.
Makes two 17- ounce loaves

    1 envelope active dry yeast
    1 cup very warm water
1½ cups SOURDOUGH STARTER *(recipe follows)*
    2 tablespoons sugar
    2 teaspoons salt
5½ cups sifted all-purpose flour
    1 egg white
    2 tablespoons cold water

1 Sprinkle yeast into very warm water in a large bowl. (Very warm water should feel comfortably warm when dropped on wrist.) Then stir in starter, sugar and salt.

2 Beat in 2 cups of the flour until smooth. Beat in enough of the remaining flour to make a soft dough.

3 Turn out onto lightly floured pastry board. Knead until smooth and elastic, about 10 minutes, using only as much flour as needed to keep dough from sticking.

4 Place in a greased large bowl, turn to coat all over with shortening; cover with a clean towel. Let rise in a warm place, away from draft, 1 hour, or until double in bulk.

5 Punch dough down; turn out onto board; invert bowl over dough; let rest 20 minutes.

6 Grease two large cooky sheets; sprinkle with cornmeal.

7 Divide dough in half and knead each half a few times. Roll up tightly from long side, jelly-roll fashion; pinch long seam tightly to seal. Roll loaf gently back and forth with hands to taper ends. Place loaf diagonally on prepared cooky sheet.

8 Roll out second half of dough to a 28-inch strip and roll up, jelly-roll fashion, starting from a long side. Shape roll into a ring on second cooky sheet.

9 Let rise again in a warm place, away from draft, 45 minutes, or until double in bulk.

10 Make slits 2 inches apart on top of breads with a very sharp knife or razor blade. Beat egg white and cold water together in a small cup. Brush loaves.

11 Bake in hot oven (400°) 40 minutes, or until golden and loaves give a hollow sound when tapped. Remove from cooky sheets to wire racks; cool completely.

SOURDOUGH STARTER

Makes 4 cups of starter

2 cups milk
2 cups sifted all-purpose flour

Pour milk into a glass or ceramic bowl and cover bowl with cheesecloth. Let stand in the outdoors for 1 day. Stir in flour and recover bowl with cheesecloth. Place outside for 2 days. Place bowl in a sunny spot indoors and allow to stand until mixture bubbles and starts to sour, about 2 days. Spoon into a quart jar with a screw cap and store in refrigerator at least 1 day before using. (If top of starter should start to dry out at any time during this process, stir in a little lukewarm water.) When you remove 1½ cups of sourdough starter, simply combine ¾ cup milk and ¾ cup flour and stir into jar. Cover jar with cheesecloth and place in sunny spot for 1 day. Remove cheesecloth; cover jar and return to refrigerator.

YEAST BREAD KNOW-HOW

Here are some hints—to help you turn out perfect bread the first time, and every time you bake it.

- *Dissolve active dry yeast in very warm water. It should register between 105° F. and 115° F. (about as hot as you'd want it for a bath). But if you're using compressed yeast, the water should only be lukewarm.*
- *To determine whether yeast is alive, "proof" it: dissolve yeast and a pinch of sugar in very warm water. The mixture should bubble. If it doesn't, stop. Start again with fresh yeast.*
- *After the yeast is "proofed," don't add other hot liquids, only lukewarm ingredients.*
- *Don't worry about kneading dough too long. You can't hurt dough by over-kneading it—but kneading too little can prevent it from rising properly. If you stop kneading, cover the dough with an inverted bowl. As soon as possible, continue to knead for the remaining time.*
- *Put kneaded dough in a thoroughly greased bowl; turn the dough over in bowl to cover all surfaces. If dough isn't properly greased (and bowl completely covered), a crusty surface will form and you'll find pebble-like particles in finished bread.*

If you don't use cloth towels, cover bowl or bowls loosely with plastic wrap.

- *Let dough rise in warm place. One of the best places is oven of gas or electric range. Place a pan of hot water on shelf under bowl of dough and close door. If there is a pilot light, leave door open.*
- *For a glossy crust on bread, brush top lightly with a mixture of either one whole egg, an egg yolk, or egg white, plus 1 or 2 tablespoons of water—immediately before baking. For a soft crust, brush lightly with melted butter or margarine as you remove bread from oven.*
- *Many bread recipes in this chapter indicate you should test for doneness by tapping top of baked item with your knuckles, and listening for a hollow sound. That's important. You shouldn't go by color alone, particularly if you're using a glass loaf pan. A nice brown crust may be covering still unbaked bread.*
- *Cool baked breads and rolls on wire racks far enough apart to allow air circulation. Also, avoid drafts; otherwise crusts may crack.*
- *To reheat bread, place loaves in a brown paper bag; sprinkle bag with a few drops of water; close tightly. Heat in moderate oven (350°) 10 minutes.*

Grandmother's White Bread

Golden crust, soft texture—delicious plain or toasted

Bake at 400° for 40 minutes.
Makes 2 loaves.

1 envelope active dry yeast
½ cup very warm water
3 tablespoons sugar
2 cups milk
2 tablespoons butter or margarine
1 tablespoon salt
6 or 7 cups sifted unbleached all-purpose flour
   OR: 7 to 8 cups sifted all-purpose flour

1 Sprinkle yeast into very warm water in a 1-cup measure; stir in ½ teaspoon of the sugar. (Very warm water should feel comfortably warm when dropped on the wrist.) Stir until yeast dissolves. Let stand, undisturbed, to proof until bubbly and double in volume, about 10 minutes.

2 Combine remaining sugar, milk, butter and salt in a small saucepan; heat just until butter melts. Pour into large bowl; cool to lukewarm. Stir in yeast.

3 Stir in 3 cups of the flour; beat until smooth. Gradually stir in enough flour to make a soft dough (3 cups if you are using unbleached flour; 4 cups if you are using all-purpose flour).

4 Turn out onto lightly floured surface; knead until smooth and elastic, about 10 minutes, using additional flour as needed to keep dough from sticking.

5 Place in a buttered bowl; turn to bring buttered side up. Cover with a towel. Let rise in a warm place, away from drafts, 1 hour, or until double in bulk.

6 Punch dough down; turn out onto lightly

floured surface, knead a few times; invert the bowl over dough; let rest 10 minutes.

7 Divide dough in half and knead each half a few times. Shape into 2 loaves. Place loaves in two buttered 8½x4½x2½-inch loaf pans.

8 Let rise again in a warm place, away from drafts, 1 hour, or until double in bulk.

9 Bake in a hot oven (400°) 40 minutes, or until golden brown and loaves sound hollow when tapped. If loaves are browning too quickly, cover loosely with foil. Remove from pans to wire racks to cool completely.

Cuban Bread

Crisp on the outside, even textured on the inside. Best to freeze the second loaf if you don't plan to serve it within two days

Bake, starting in cold oven,
400° for 40 minutes.
Makes two 17½-ounce loaves

1 envelope active dry yeast
2 cups very warm water
2 tablespoons sugar
3 teaspoons salt
6 cups sifted all-purpose flour
  Cornmeal
  Ice water

1 Sprinkle yeast into very warm water in a large bowl. (Very warm water should feel comfortably warm when dropped on wrist.) Stir until yeast dissolves, then stir in sugar and salt.

2 Beat in 2 cups of the flour until smooth. Beat in enough of the remaining flour to make a soft dough.

3 Turn out onto a lightly floured pastry board. Knead until smooth and elastic, about 5 minutes, using only as much flour as needed to keep dough from sticking.

4 Place in a greased large bowl, turn to coat all over with shortening; cover with a clean towel. Let rise in a warm place, away from draft, 1 hour, or until double in bulk.

5 Punch dough down; turn out onto board; invert bowl over dough; allow to rest 10 minutes.

6 Divide dough in half and knead each piece a few times. Roll out each piece to a 15x10-inch rectangle. Roll up tightly from long side, jelly-roll fashion; pinch long seam tightly to seal. Roll loaf gently back and forth to taper ends. Place loaf diagonally on a large cooky sheet which has been greased, then sprinkled with cornmeal.

7 Pat out second piece of dough to an 8-inch round and place on a second prepared cooky sheet.

8 Let rise again in a warm place, away from draft, 45 minutes, or until double in bulk.

9 Make slits 2 inches apart on top of loaves with a very sharp knife or razor blade; make crisscross slits, 2 inches apart, on round loaf. Brush all with ice water.

10 Place cooky sheets in cold oven.

11 Turn oven to hot (400°); bake 40 minutes, brushing several times with ice water, or until bread gives a hollow sound when tapped. Remove from cooky sheets to wire racks; cool completely.

You'll have to check the index for some of these off-beat breads, but the effort is worth it. (Clockwise from top), **Cuban Bread** loaves, **Sourdough, Hi-Protein Bread,** sesame-studded **Armenian Bread, Two-Tone Rye Twist, White Bread,** and (round) **Cuban Bread.**

Two luscious breads that test your culinary skills: **Sesame Twist** (see index for recipe) and **Golden Brioche.**

Golden Brioche

A giant-sized bread—cut off a slice and butter generously

Bake at 400° for 50 minutes.
Makes one 9-inch loaf.

½ cup milk
¾ cup (1½ sticks) butter or margarine
¼ cup sugar
1 teaspoon salt
1 envelope active dry yeast
¼ cup very warm water
4 eggs
4 cups sifted all-purpose flour

1 Scald milk in a small saucepan; cool to luke-warm.

2 Cream butter or margarine until fluffy-light in a large bowl; beat in sugar and salt.

3 Sprinkle yeast into very warm water in a cup. (Very warm water should feel comfortably warm when dropped on wrist.) Stir until yeast dissolves, then beat, a little at a time, into butter mixture; beat in milk until well-blended.

4 Beat eggs until creamy-thick in a small bowl; measure 2 tablespoonfuls into a cup; cover and chill for brushing loaf in Step 9. Beat remaining into butter mixture until well-blended.

5 Beat in flour, 1 cup at a time, until smooth, then continue beating 10 minutes. (Dough will be heavy and sticky.) Cover with a clean towel. Let rise in a warm place, away from draft, 2 hours, or until double in bulk.

6 Stir dough down; cover again; chill overnight.

7 When ready to shape, stir dough down again; turn out onto a very lightly floured pastry cloth or board; shape into an oval about 8 inches long. Cut off slightly less than ¼ of the dough and set aside to make the topknot.

8 Shape remaining dough into a smooth ball; place in a buttered 9-inch brioche pan or 8-cup round baking dish. Cut a deep 3-inch cross in center with a sharp knife; pull points upward and out with a knife to make a hollow for top.

9 Shape saved dough into a "pear;" place, narrow end down, in hollow in top of large ball. Tuck points in to make a smooth edge; cover. Let rise again, in a warm place, away from draft, 2 hours, or until double in bulk. Brush all over with saved beaten egg.

10 Bake in hot oven (400°) 50 minutes, until loaf is richly golden and gives a hollow sound when tapped. Remove from pan; cool on a wire rack.

White Bread

(Rapid-mix method)
Golden brown slices just pull apart for easy serving

Bake at 400° for 30 minutes.
Makes two 21-ounce loaves

5½ cups sifted all-purpose flour
1 envelope active dry yeast
3 tablespoons sugar
2 teaspoons salt
1½ cups water
½ cup milk
3 tablespoons vegetable oil
¼ cup (½ stick) butter or margarine, melted

1 Mix 2 cups of the flour, yeast, sugar and salt in a large bowl.

2 Heat water, milk and oil in a small saucepan until very warm to the touch (not scalding); add to flour. Beat with electric mixer at medium speed 2 minutes, scraping bowl several times.

3 Blend in ¾ cup more flour at low speed, then beat at high speed for 3 minutes. Stir in remaining flour to make a soft dough.

4 Turn out onto a lightly floured pastry board and knead until smooth and elastic, about 10 minutes, using only as much flour as needed to keep dough from sticking. Place in a greased large bowl; turn to coat all over with shortening; cover with a clean towel. Let rise in a warm place, away from draft, for 1½ hours, or until it has doubled in bulk.

5 Punch dough down; turn out onto lightly floured pastry board; invert bowl over dough; allow to rest 10 minutes.

6 Divide dough in half and knead each half several times. Roll out each half to a 16x8-inch rectangle. Roll up firmly from short side, jelly-roll fashion. Cut roll into 12 slices. Brush each slice with melted butter or margarine; stack slices to reshape as loaf in a greased 8½x4½x2½-inch loaf pan. (Turn loaf pan on a short side and rest against back of counter for ease of stacking slices in pan.)

7 Let rise again in a warm place, away from draft, 1 hour, or until double in bulk.

8 Bake in hot oven (400°) 30 minutes, or until golden and loaves give a hollow sound when tapped. Remove from the pans to wire racks and then cool completely.

HOW TO MAKE YEAST DOUGH

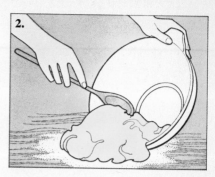

1. While yeast is proofing, sift flour and measure onto wax paper; place heated milk and/or water, sugar or syrup, salt and butter or shortening called for in recipe in a large bowl; cool. Add proofed yeast to bowl.

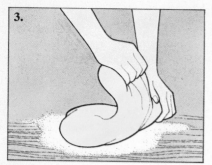

2. Stir in flour, according to recipe directions; beat with a wooden spoon until dough is smooth. Gradually add enough of remaining flour until dough forms a soft ball and no longer clings to side of bowl. Turn out onto a floured surface.

3. With floured hands, pick up far edge of dough and fold toward you.

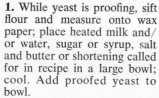

4. Push into the dough, away from you, with heel of one hand, and at the same time, give the dough a quarter of a turn by pulling it toward you with the other hand. Repeat folding, pushing and turning this way, adding just enough flour to keep dough from sticking, until dough feels smooth and elastic.

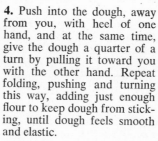

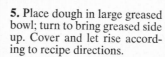

5. Place dough in large greased bowl; turn to bring greased side up. Cover and let rise according to recipe directions.

6. When dough has doubled in bulk, press with two fingers; if indentations stay, dough is ready.

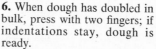

7. Punch down dough with fist. Then, turn out onto a lightly floured surface and knead according to recipe directions.

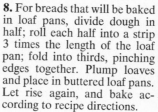

8. For breads that will be baked in loaf pans, divide dough in half; roll each half into a strip 3 times the length of the loaf pan; fold into thirds, pinching edges together. Plump loaves and place in buttered loaf pans. Let rise again, and bake according to recipe directions.

Hearty Wheat Bread

A plump loaf of this wonderful homemade specialty plus a glass or two of jelly make a thoughtful remembrance

Bake regular-size loaves at 350° for 1 hour, or large round loaf at 375° for 1 hour.
Makes 2 regular-size loaves or one 9-inch round loaf.

2 cups milk
¼ cup molasses
3 tablespoons butter or margarine
3 teaspoons salt
2 envelopes active dry yeast
½ cup very warm water
5 cups sifted all-purpose flour
2 cups uncooked granulated whole-wheat cereal

1 Scald milk with molasses, butter or margarine and salt in a small saucepan; cool to lukewarm.
2 Sprinkle yeast into very warm water in a large bowl. (Very warm water should feel comfortably warm when dropped on wrist.) Stir until yeast dissolves, then stir in cooled milk mixture.
3 Beat in 2 cups of the flour until smooth; stir in cereal, then beat in just enough of remaining 3 cups flour to make a stiff dough.
4 Turn out onto a lightly floured pastry cloth or board; knead until smooth and elastic, adding only enough extra flour to keep dough from sticking.
5 Place in a greased large bowl, turning to coat all over with shortening; cover with a clean towel. Let rise in a warm place, away from draft, 1 hour, or until double in bulk. Punch dough down; knead a few times.
6 To make 2 regular-size loaves: Divide dough in half; roll out, half at a time, to a rectangle, 18x6; roll up, jelly-roll fashion. Place each, seam side down, in a greased loaf pan, 9x5x3; cover.
7 To make one 9-inch round loaf: Shape dough into a 9-inch round and place in a 9-inch spring-form pan; cover.
8 Let either size rise again in a warm place, away from draft, 30 minutes, or until double in bulk.
9 Bake regular-size loaves in moderate oven (350°) 1 hour, or until richly golden and bread gives a hollow sound when tapped. Bake large round loaf in moderate oven (375°) 1 hour, or until richly browned and bread gives a hollow sound when tapped.
10 Loosen loaves around edges with a knife; turn out onto wire racks. Brush tops lightly with butter or margarine, if you prefer a soft crust. Cool bread completely.

BREAD DECORATING IDEAS

What could be simpler than sprinkling loaf with a snowy shower of 10X (confectioners' powdered) sugar? Yet it looks so festive! (Just press the sugar through a fine sieve right onto bread.) Or trim with sliced almonds (buy them in packages) arranged, petal fashion, around whole or halved candied cherries. Another flower idea: Cut stems and leaves from thin slices of candied citron or bright green gumdrops; use cherries for the blossoms.

Buttermilk Wheat Bread

Creamy buttermilk blends with nutritious flour and crunchy cracked wheat

Bake at 375° for 40 minutes.
Makes 2 loaves.

2 envelopes active dry yeast
½ cup very warm water
2 cups buttermilk
2 tablespoons vegetable shortening
¼ cup honey
1 tablespoon salt
½ teaspoon baking soda
3½ cups whole wheat flour
1 cup cracked wheat
2¼ cups sifted all-purpose flour

(continued)

1 Sprinkle yeast into very warm water in a 1-cup measure; stir in 1 teaspoon of the honey. (Very warm water should feel comfortably warm when dropped on wrist.) Stir until yeast dissolves. Let stand undisturbed to proof until bubbly and double in volume, about 10 minutes.

2 Heat buttermilk with shortening, remaining honey and salt in small saucepan just to luke-warm; combine with yeast mixture in a large bowl.

3 Stir in baking soda, whole wheat flour and cracked wheat until smooth; beat in enough of the all-purpose flour to make a soft dough.

4 Turn out onto lightly floured surface. Knead until smooth and elastic; about 10 minutes, using only as much flour as needed to keep dough from sticking.

5 Place in a buttered bowl; turn to bring buttered side up. Cover with a towel. Let rise in a warm place, away from drafts, 1 hour, or until double in bulk.

6 Punch dough down; turn out onto lightly floured surface; knead a few times; invert a bowl over dough; let rest 10 minutes.

7 Divide dough in half and knead each half a few times. Roll each piece to an 18x9-inch rectangle. Roll up from short side, jelly roll fashion. Pinch ends together with fingers to seal. Place each loaf seam side down in a greased 9x5x3-inch pan.

8 Let rise again in a warm place, away from drafts, 40 minutes, or until double in bulk.

9 Bake in moderate oven (375°) 35 minutes, or until golden brown and loaves sound hollow when tapped. Remove from pans to wire racks to cool completely.

Double-Wheat Whole Wheat Bread

Whole wheat bread at its best; hearty flavor, golden color—with honey and wheat germ for extra goodness and nutrition

Bake at 400° for 40 minutes.
Makes 2 loaves.

2 envelopes active dry yeast
1 cup very warm water
⅓ cup honey
2 cups milk
¼ cup (½ stick) butter or margarine
1½ tablespoons salt
5 cups whole wheat flour
¼ cup wheat germ
3 cups sifted all-purpose flour

1 Sprinkle yeast into very warm water in a 1-cup measure; stir in 1 teaspoon of the honey. (Very warm water should feel comfortably warm when dropped on wrist.) Stir until yeast dissolves. Let stand, undisturbed, to proof until bubbly and double in volume, about 10 minutes.

2 Combine remaining honey with milk, butter or margarine and salt in a small saucepan; heat until butter melts. Pour into large bowl; cool to lukewarm. Stir in yeast mixture.

3 Stir in whole wheat flour and wheat germ until smooth; add enough all-purpose flour to make a soft dough.

4 Turn out onto lightly floured surface. Knead until smooth and elastic, about 10 minutes, using only as much flour as needed to keep dough from sticking.

5 Place dough in a buttered large bowl; turn to bring buttered side up. Cover with towel. Let rise in a warm place, away from drafts, 1 hour, or until double in bulk.

6 Punch dough down; turn out onto lightly floured surface; knead a few times; invert bowl over dough; let rest about 10 minutes.

7 Divide dough in half and knead each half a few times; shape into 2 loaves. Place loaves in two buttered 9x5x3-inch loaf pans.

8 Let rise in a warm place, away from drafts, 45 minutes, or until double in bulk.

9 Bake in a hot oven (400°) 40 minutes, or until browned and loaves sound hollow when tapped. Remove from pans to wire racks to cool completely.

High-Protein Whole-Wheat Bread

This special bread is super-high in protein. Here's a great way to increase the nutritional value of bread

Bake at 375° for 35 minutes.
Makes 2 loaves.

2 envelopes active dry yeast
3 tablespoons sugar
1½ cups very warm water
1 cup milk
2 tablespoons butter or margarine
1 tablespoon salt
⅔ cup instant nonfat dry milk
⅓ cup soya bean powder
3 tablespoons wheat germ
3 cups whole wheat flour
3 cups sifted unbleached all-purpose flour
Slightly beaten egg
Sesame seeds

When you want toast, you can't beat homemade bread. When cool, these breads slice neatly without "crumbling"—just what you need to pop in the toaster.

1 Sprinkle yeast into ½ cup of the very warm water in a 1 cup measure; stir in 1 teaspoon of the sugar. (Very warm water should feel comfortably warm when dropped on wrist.) Stir until yeast dissolves. Let stand, undisturbed, to proof 10 minutes, or until bubbly and double in volume.

2 Combine remaining water and sugar with milk, butter or margarine and salt in a small saucepan; heat until butter melts. Pour into large bowl; cool to lukewarm. Stir in yeast.

3 Stir in dry milk powder, soya bean powder, wheat germ, 1½ cups of the whole wheat flour and 1 cup of all-purpose flour. Beat at medium speed with electric mixer, 3 minutes, scraping down side of bowl several times. Stir in remaining whole wheat flour and 1 cup all-purpose flour to make a stiff dough.

4 Turn out onto lightly floured surface. Knead until smooth and elastic, about 10 minutes, using the remaining all-purpose flour in order to keep the dough from sticking.

5 Place in a buttered large bowl; turn to bring buttered side up. Cover with a towel. Let rise in a warm place, away from drafts, 1 to 1½ hours, or until double in bulk.

6 Punch dough down; turn out onto lightly floured surface; knead a few times; invert bowl
(continued)

over dough; let rest about 10 minutes. Divide dough in half and knead each piece a few times; shape into 2 loaves. Place in two buttered 8½x4½x2½-inch loaf pans.

7 Let rise again in a warm place, away from drafts, 45 minutes, or until double in bulk. Brush tops with beaten egg; sprinkle with sesame seeds.

8 Bake in a moderate oven (375°) 35 minutes, or until golden and loaves sound hollow when tapped. Remove from pans to wire racks; cool completely.

Note: If you wish to make rolls, divide dough into 16 even pieces; shape into round balls for hamburger rolls, or 5-inch-long fingers for frankfurter rolls. Place, 3 inches apart, on greased large cooky sheet. Let rise 30 to 40 minutes, or until double in bulk. Brush tops with egg; sprinkle with sesame seeds. Bake in a hot oven (400°) 15 to 20 minutes, or until golden brown.

rise in a warm place, away from drafts, 1 hour, or until double in bulk.

5 Butter a large cookie sheet. Sprinkle with cornmeal.

6 Punch dough down; turn onto lightly floured surface; knead a few times; invert bowl over dough; let rest 10 minutes; divide dough in half and knead each half a few times. Shape into 2 loaves. Place at least 4 inches apart on prepared cookie sheet.

7 Let rise again in a warm place, away from drafts, 45 minutes, or until double in bulk. Brush tops with water.

8 Bake in a hot oven (400°) 35 minutes, or until browned and loaves sound hollow when tapped. Remove from cookie sheet to wire rack; cool completely.

Scandinavian Rye Bread

A traditional Northern European favorite, chock full of savory caraway seeds

Bake at 400° for 35 minutes.
Makes 2 loaves.

2 envelopes active dry yeast
2½ cups very warm water
¼ cup light molasses
4 teaspoons salt
2 tablespoons shortening
2½ cups rye flour
1 tablespoon caraway seeds, crushed
5½ to 6 cups sifted all-purpose flour
Cornmeal

1 Sprinkle yeast into ½ cup of the very warm water; stir in 1 teaspoon of the molasses. (Very warm water should feel comfortably warm when dropped on wrist.) Stir until yeast dissolves. Let stand, undisturbed, to proof until bubbly and double in volume, about 10 minutes.

2 Combine remaining water and molasses with salt and shortening in a large bowl; stir in yeast mixture, rye flour and caraway seeds; add enough all-purpose flour to make a soft dough.

3 Turn out onto a lightly floured surface. Knead until smooth and elastic, about 10 minutes, using enough of the remaining flour to keep dough from sticking.

4 Place in buttered large bowl; turn dough to bring buttered side up; cover with towel. Let

Swedish Limpa

This orange-scented whole rye and wheat bread has been a Scandinavian favorite for many generations

Bake at 375° for 45 minutes.
Makes 2 loaves.

2 envelopes active dry yeast
2½ cups very warm water
¼ cup firmly packed brown sugar
⅓ cup molasses
3 tablespoons vegetable shortening
1 tablespoon salt
2 tablespoons grated orange rind
1 teaspoon anise seeds, crushed with hammer
1 cup cracked wheat
3½ cups whole rye flour
3¾ to 4 cups sifted unbleached all-purpose flour

1 Sprinkle yeast into ½ cup of the very warm water; stir in 1 teaspoon of the brown sugar. (Very warm water should feel comfortably warm when dropped on wrist.) Stir until yeast dissolves. Let stand, undisturbed, to proof until bubbly and double in volume, about 10 minutes.

2 Combine remaining water and sugar with molasses, shortening and salt in a small saucepan. Heat until shortening melts; cool to lukewarm.

3 Combine yeast mixture and molasses mixture

in large bowl. Add orange ring, anise seeds, cracked wheat and rye flour. Beat with electric mixer at medium speed for 3 minutes. Gradually stir in enough all-purpose flour to make a soft dough.

4 Turn out onto lightly floured surface; knead until smooth and elastic, using remaining all-purpose flour to keep dough from sticking; add more flour, if needed.

5 Place in buttered large bowl; turn to bring greased side up; cover with a towel or plastic wrap. Let rise in a warm place, away from drafts, 1½ hours, or until double in bulk.

6 Punch dough down; turn out onto lightly floured surface; invert bowl over dough; allow to rest 10 minutes. Divide dough in half and knead each half a few times, then shape each into an oval loaf. Place on buttered cookie sheets.

7 Let rise in a warm place, away from drafts, 40 minutes, or until double in bulk.

8 Bake in moderate oven (375°) 45 minutes, or until golden brown and loaves sound hollow when tapped. Cool loaves on wire racks.

Note: For an interesting variation, shape each half of dough into a round. Glaze by brushing tops with a mixture of 1 slightly beaten egg white plus 1 tablespoon cold water.

Carioca Pinwheel Loaf

Chocolate and spice go round and round in this brown-and-gold loaf

Bake at 375° for 30 minutes.
Makes 1 loaf.

½ cup milk
4 tablespoons (½ stick) butter or margarine
¼ cup sugar
1 teaspoon salt
1 package active dry yeast
¼ cup very warm water
2 eggs, beaten
3 cups sifted all-purpose flour
1 square unsweetened chocolate, melted
½ teaspoon cinnamon
  Syrup Glaze (recipe follows)

1 Scald milk with butter or margarine in small saucepan; stir in sugar and salt; cool to luke-

2 Dissolve yeast in very warm water in large bowl. (Very warm water should feel comfortably warm when dropped on wrist.) Stir in cooled milk mixture and beaten eggs.

3 Stir in 2 cups flour; beat until smooth. Gradually stir in enough of remaining flour to make a stiff dough.

4 Divide dough in half; turn out one half onto lightly floured pastry cloth or board. (Leave remaining half of dough in bowl for mixing with chocolate and cinnamon in Step 6.) Knead until smooth and elastic, adding only enough flour to keep from sticking.

5 Place dough in greased medium-size bowl; cover with clean towel; let rise in warm place, away from draft, 1 hour, or until double in bulk.

6 Stir melted chocolate and cinnamon into remaining dough. (Do not worry if it is marbled, for chocolate will melt during baking.) Knead and let rise, as in Steps 4 and 5 above.

(continued)

After you've spent some time in the kitchen baking bread, your family will be delighted when you produce twin-dough **Carioca Pinwheel Loaf.**

7 Punch both doughs down; roll out half of plain dough to ⅛-inch thickness on lightly floured pastry cloth or board. Cut into a rectangle. 10x8; lay on sheet of wax paper. Save dough cuttings for Step 9.

8 Roll out half of chocolate dough and cut the same as plain dough; place rectangle on top of plain dough; save cuttings for Step 9. Repeat Steps 7 and 8 with other halves of plain and chocolate doughs to make a total of 4 layers, ending with chocolate.

9 Roll chocolate cuttings into a rope, 8 inches long. Roll plain cuttings into a rectangle, 8x4; wrap around chocolate rope; place on one end of stacked layers. Roll up, as for jelly roll, starting at rope end.

10 Place, seam side down, in greased loaf pan, 9x5x3; make 4 shallow diagonal cuts in top of loaf. Cover with clean towel; let rise in warm place, away from draft, 1 hour, or until double in bulk.

11 Bake in moderate oven (375°) 30 minutes, or until loaf is golden-brown and gives a hollow sound when tapped; remove from pan. Brush with *Syrup Glaze*; cool on wire rack.

SYRUP GLAZE

Combine ½ cup light corn syrup and ¼ cup water in small heavy saucepan; heat slowly to a rolling boil; boil 1 minute. Store any remaining glaze in covered jar. Heat just before using. Makes ½ cup.

Vienna Crescent

This bread is made with the "sponge" method, which gives a fine texture inside and a lovely brown crust outside

Bake at 450° for 10 minutes, then at 350° for 30 mintues for crescent, 40 minutes for loaf.
Makes 1 crescent and 1 loaf

 2 envelopes active dry yeast
 1 cup very warm water
 4 teaspoons sugar
 6 cups sifted all-purpose flour
1½ cups cold milk
 3 teaspoons salt
 1 egg, slightly beaten
 Poppy seeds

1 Make "sponge": Sprinkle yeast into very warm water in a large bowl. (Very warm water should feel comfortably warm when dropped on wrist.) Stir until yeast dissolves.

2 Stir in 1 teaspoon sugar and 2 cups of the flour; beat until smooth. Cover bowl with plastic wrap or foil. Let rise in a warm place away from draft 2½ to 3 hours, or until large bubbles appear on the surface.

3 Stir in milk, remaining sugar, salt and 2 cups flour; beat until smooth; gradually add remaining flour. Turn out onto lightly floured pastry board; knead until smooth and elastic, about 5 minutes, using only as much flour as needed to keep dough from sticking.

4 Place in a greased large bowl; turn to coat all over with shortening; cover with clean towel. Let rise in warm place, away from draft, 1 hour, or until double in bulk.

5 Punch dough down; turn out onto board; knead 1 minute; divide in half. For crescent: Roll one half into a 30x24x24-inch triangle; roll up from long side to opposite point. Transfer to greased cooky sheet; shape into crescent. For loaf: Pinch off about 2 tablespoons dough from other half of dough and set aside for decoration; shape remaining dough into an 8-inch loaf. Place loaf on greased cooky sheet. With palms of hands, roll reserved dough into a 10-inch-long strip; place strip on top of loaf, folding it under at both ends. Cover; let rise again in a warm place, away from draft, 45 minutes, or until double in bulk.

6 Brush tops with slightly beaten egg; sprinkle with poppy seeds.

7 Bake in very hot oven (450°) 10 minutes, lower heat to 350° and bake 30 minutes longer for crescent and 35 to 40 minutes longer for loaf, or until breads give a hollow sound when tapped. Remove from cooky sheets to wire racks; cool completely.

100% Whole-Wheat Bread

A lovely brown-flecked and plump loaf, this 100% whole-wheat bread rises above the pan level to demonstrate that this grain has almost the same gluten power as white flour

Bake at 375° for 40 minutes.
Makes 3 loaves.

 9 to 10 cups whole-wheat flour (approximately)
 4 teaspoons salt
 2 envelopes active dry yeast
1½ cups milk
1½ cups water
 ½ cup honey
 6 tablespoons (¾ stick) butter or margarine

1 *Preparation: 15 minutes.* Thoroughly blend 3 cups of the whole-wheat flour, the salt and yeast in a large mixing bowl. Heat milk, water, honey and butter in a medium-size saucepan until lukewarm; gradually add to dry ingredients in bowl, and beat at medium speed with electric mixer for 2 minutes, scraping bowl once or twice. Add 1 cup more of flour, or enough to make a thick batter. Beat at high speed for 3 minutes. Stop the mixer and add additional flour, stirring with a spoon; then stir by hand, until a soft mass forms.

2 *Resting: 10 minutes.* Turn the soft dough onto a lighly floured work surface, invert the mixing bowl over the dough to cover, and let dough rest 10 minutes.

3 *Kneading: 8 minutes.* Knead the dough until it is smooth and elastic, adding ¼ cup or more additional flour if the dough is moist or slack. Knead for about 8 minutes (5 minutes if using the dough hook of an electric mixer).

4 *First Rising: 50 minutes.* Press dough into a large greased bowl. Cover the top tightly with foil or plastic wrap and move to a warm draft-free place till dough doubles in volume.

5 *Shaping: 10 minutes.* Punch dough down; turn out on work surface; divide into thirds and shape each third into a loaf. This can be done by flattening each piece into an oval, folding in half, pinching the seam tightly and placing seam side down, in 8½x4½-inch loaf pan. Repeat with remaining thirds.

6 *Second Rising: 50 minutes.* Cover the pans with wax paper and let the loaves rise in a warm place until they have doubled in volume, and the centers have risen about 1 inch above the level of the edge of the pans.

7 *Baking: 40 minutes.* Bake in a moderate oven (375°) for 40 minutes or until they test done when thumped on the bottom crust. If they do not sound hard and hollow, return to the oven without the pans for an additional 10 minutes.

8 *Final Step:* Let cool on metal rack, out of pans. Brush with butter.

Corn Bubble Bread

Cornmeal gives this loaf a nice coarse texture, but it is the stacking of the small balls of dough in a tube pan that gives it its bubbles. The loaf can be sliced, or each bubble can be pulled off

Bake at 375° for 55 minutes.
Makes one large round loaf.

5 cups sifted all-purpose flour (approximately)
2 tablespoons sugar

1 tablespoon salt
2 cups yellow cornmeal
2 packages active dry yeast
1¾ cups milk
½ cup water
3 tablespoons vegetable shortening
2 tablespoons melted butter or margarine

1 *Preparation: 20 minutes.* Blend 2 cups of the flour, the sugar, salt, cornmeal and yeast in a large bowl. Heat milk, water and shortening in a medium-size saucepan until lukewarm. Pour into the dry ingredients and beat at medium-speed with electric mixer for 2 minutes. Add about ½ cup more flour to make the batter thick. Beat at high speed for 2 minutes, scraping down sides of the bowl twice during the beating. (Beating can also be done by hand.) Beat with a wooden spoon, for approximately the same length of time or until the batter pulls away from the sides of the bowl in strands. Turn off mixer, stir in additional flour to make a rough mass that can be worked with hands.

2 *Kneading: 8 minutes.* Turn the dough onto a lightly floured work surface and knead with a strong push-turn-fold action. (The dough will be smooth and elastic, and feel "alive" under your hands.) Knead for about 8 minutes (5 if using dough hook of electric mixer).

3 *Resting: 20 minutes.* Cover the ball of dough with the bowl inverted, and let rest 20 minutes.

4. *Shaping: 20 minutes.* Uncover the dough, punch it down and knead briefly to collapse the air pockets. Divide the dough into 32 small pieces. (The quickest and most accurate way is to divide the dough with a knife into 2-4-8-16-32 pieces successively.) Roll into balls between the palms of your hands. Arrange half of balls into a layer in a greased 10-inch tube pan. (They will not necessarily touch.) Arrange the remaining 16 balls in a layer on top. (Any irregularity of form will be lost when the loaf rises.) Brush with part of the butter. Cover and let rise in a warm, draft-free place for 1 hour. Puncture any gas bubbles that have pushed out from the surface of the loaf with a greased wooden pick.

5 *Baking: 55 minutes.* Bake in a moderate oven (375°) for 55 minutes. When the loaf is brown and tapping on the bottom crust yields a hard and hollow sound, it is done. If it is still soft, return to the oven without the pan for an additional 10 minutes.

6 *Final step.* Let cool on metal rack, out of pan. Brush with remaining melted butter.

Old Milwaukee Rye Bread

This is a two- or three-day affair that produces a fine rye loaf

Bake at 375° for 40 minutes.
Makes 2 to 3 loaves.

1 envelope active dry yeast
1½ cups very warm water
2 cups whole rye flour
2 tablespoons caraway seeds
1 envelope active dry yeast
1 cup very warm water
¼ cup molasses
1 egg, at room temperature
1 tablespoon salt
1 cup whole rye flour
5½ to 6 cups sifted all-purpose flour
3 tablespoons vegetable shortening
1 egg
1 tablespoon milk

1 *Sponge preparation: 1 to 3 days.* Dissolve 1 envelope of the yeast in the 1½ cups very warm water in a large bowl. (Very warm water should feel comfortably warm when dropped on the wrist.) Stir in the 2 cups rye flour and 1 tablespoon of the caraway seeds. (This is called the sponge.) Cover the bowl snugly with plastic wrap so that the sponge loses none of the moisture that condenses on the plastic and drops back into the mixture. The dark brown paste will rise and fall the first day as it develops flavor and a delicious aroma. The sponge, which resembles a wet mash that is too thick to pour and too thin to knead, can be used anytime after 12 hours, although the longer it stands the better the flavor—up to three days.
2 *Bake Day Preparation: 20 minutes.* Uncover the sponge bowl, sprinkle on the remaining envelope of yeast, and add the remaining warm water. Blend well with 25 strokes of a wooden spoon. Add molasses, remaining caraway seeds, egg, salt, remaining rye flour and about 2 cups of the all-purpose flour. Beat until smooth, about 100 strokes. Add shortening. Stir in the remaining flour, first with the spoon and then by hand. The dough should clean the side of the bowl, although it will be sticky because of the rye flour.
3 *Kneading: 5 minutes.* Turn the dough out on a floured counter top or pastry board. Knead it about 200 times or until the dough is smooth; about 5 minutes. (Light sprinkles of flour will keep the dough from sticking.) The dough must be firm. It may sag slightly if left for a moment or two, but should not collapse. If it does collapse, knead in more flour.

4 *First Rising: 1 hour, 10 minutes.* Return the dough to the large bowl; pat top with soft butter or shortening, and replace plastic wrap. Leave in warm place for about 1 hour, or until dough has doubled in volume. Punch dough down and let rest 10 minutes.
5 *Shaping: 20 minutes.* Turn dough out onto work surface. To make two round loaves: Divide dough in half. Shape each half into a smooth ball, and place on greased cookie sheets. To make long slender loaves: divide dough in thirds. Roll out one portion to a long rectangle with floured rolling pin. Starting at one long edge, roll up tightly and pinch together firmly at the seam. Place these long loaves side by side on greased cookie sheet, 2 inches in between.
6 *Second Rising: 40 minutes.* Cover the loaves with wax paper supported on glass tumblers so paper does not touch dough. Return to warm place for about 40 minutes, or until loaves have doubled in volume.
7 *Baking: 40 minutes.* Carefully make 3 or 4 diagonal slashes on top of each loaf with a sharp razor. Brush the loaves with the remaining egg mixed with the milk for a shiny crust. Sprinkle the wet glaze with caraway seeds. Bake the loaves in a moderate oven (375°) for about 40 minutes or until they sound' hollow when thumped on the bottom crust. If the loaves appear to be browning too quickly, cover with a piece of foil or brown grocery bag.
8 *Final Step.* Remove loaves from oven to wire racks. Cool completely. This bread keeps for at least a week or more—and freezes well.

Challah

The serving of this golden egg bread traditionally marks the beginning of the Jewish Sabbath

Bake at 350° for 30 minutes.
Makes 2 braided loaves.

1½ cups water
¼ cup sugar
3 teaspoons salt
⅓ cup butter or margarine
2 envelopes active dry yeast
½ cup very warm water
3 eggs
7½ cups sifted all-purpose flour
1 tablespoon water
Shortening
2 teaspoons poppy seeds

1 Combine water, sugar, salt and butter or margarine in a small saucepan. Heat slowly until butter or margarine melts: cool to lukewarm.

2 Beat eggs in a small bowl. Reserve 2 tablespoons for Step 8.

3 Sprinkle yeast into very warm water in a large bowl. (Very warm water should feel comfortably warm when dropped on the wrist.) Stir until the yeast dissolves; then stir the water mixture and the eggs together.

4 Beat in 4 cups of flour until smooth. Beat in enough remaining flour to make a soft dough.

5 Turn out onto a lightly floured surface; knead until smooth and elastic, about 5 minutes, using only as much flour as needed to keep dough from sticking. The sticky soft dough will absorb flour as you knead it, and will become velvety-soft.

6 Place in a greased large bowl; turn to coat all over with shortening; cover with a clean towel. Let rise in a warm place, away from drafts, 1½ hours, or until double in bulk.

7 Punch dough down; let rise 30 minutes, or until almost double in bulk. Punch dough down again; turn out onto lightly floured surface; knead a few times; divide into 6 even pieces. Roll each into a rope about 15 inches long.

8 Place 3 ropes on a greased cookie sheet; plait into a braid; fasten securely at both ends. Repeat with remaining 3 ropes of dough. Let rise again in a warm place, away from drafts, 1 hour, or until double in bulk. Combine the reserved 2 tablespoons of egg and the 1 tablespoon water; brush over bread; sprinkle with poppy seeds.

9 Bake in moderate oven (350°) 30 minutes, or until braids are golden, and sound hollow when tapped. Place braids on wire racks; cool.

Hi-Protein Bread

This special bread, higher in protein, is our version of the Cornell formula for increasing the nutritional value of bread

Bake at 350° for 50 minutes.
Makes two 26- ounce loaves

2 envelopes active dry yeast
2½ cups very warm water
1 cup nonfat dry milk
2 tablespoons honey
2 tablespoons vegetable oil
3 teaspoons salt
⅓ cup soya bean powder (from an
 11-ounce box)
2 tablespoons wheat germ
6½ cups sifted all-purpose flour

1 Sprinkle yeast into very warm water in a large bowl. (Very warm water should feel comfortably warm when dropped on wrist.) Stir until yeast dissolves, then stir in dry milk, honey, oil and salt.

2 Beat in soya bean powder and wheat germ with 2 cups of the flour until smooth. Beat in enough of the remaining flour to make a soft dough.

3 Turn out onto lightly floured pastry board. Knead until smooth and elastic, about 10 minutes, using only as much flour as needed to keep dough from sticking.

4 Place in a greased large bowl; turn to coat all over with shortening; cover with a clean towel. Let rise in a warm place, away from draft, 1 hour, or until double in bulk.

5 Punch dough down; turn out onto board; invert bowl over dough; allow to rest 20 minutes.

6 Divide dough in half and knead each piece a few times. Roll out each piece to an 18x9-inch rectangle. Roll up from short side, jelly-roll fashion. Press ends with hands to seal; fold under; place, seam side down, in a 9x5x3-inch greased loaf pan. Repeat with second half.

7 Let rise again in a warm place, away from draft, 40 minutes, or until double in bulk.

8 Bake in moderate oven (350°) 50 minutes, or until golden and loaves give a hollow sound when tapped. Remove from pans to wire racks; cool completely.

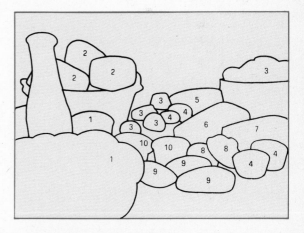

**IDENTIFICATION OF BREADS
SHOWN ON FOLLOWING PAGES**

1—**Parmesan Garlic Bread;** 2—**Cheddar Cheese Bread;** 3—**Bacon Cheese Puffs;** 4—**Rio Grande Corn Muffins;** 5—**Swiss Batter Bread;** 6—**Cheese Cranberry Bread;** 7—**Cottage Cheese Fruit Bread;** 8—**Deviled Ham and Cheese Pinwheels;** 9—**Easy Cheese Boreks;** 10—**Little Dill Cheese Loaves.**

Follow the directions and you'll soon be producing perfect breads such as these—tall, brown, and rounded with a good definition between the top and the sides.

Anadama Bread

Legend has it an old New England fisherman developed this bread from a cornmeal mush that his lazy wife, Anna, had been making for years. One day, so the story goes, the fisherman added yeast to her concoction, and, as he did so, supposedly yelled, "Anna, damn her!" The result of his efforts: A delicious new bread— "Anadama"

Bake at 375° for 50 minutes.
Makes 1 round loaf.

1½ *cups water*
 ½ *cup cornmeal*
 2 *teaspoons salt*
 6 *tablespoons butter or margarine*
 ½ *cup light molasses*
 2 *envelopes active dry yeast*
 ½ *cup very warm water*
 6 *cups sifted all-purpose flour*
    Shortening
    Cornmeal (for topping)

1 Heat water, cornmeal, salt, butter or margarine and molasses in a medium-size saucepan until thick and bubbly. Pour into a large bowl; cool to lukewarm, about 45 minutes.
2 Sprinkle yeast into ½ cup very warm water in a cup. (Very warm water should feel comfortably warm when dropped on wrist.) Stir until yeast dissolves, then blend into cooled cornmeal mixture.
3 Beat in 2 cups of the flour until smooth. Stir in 3 more cups of flour, 1 cup at a time, until dough is very stiff.
4 Turn out onto a lightly floured surface. Knead until elastic, about 10 minutes, using remaining cup of flour, as needed, to keep dough from sticking.
5 Place dough in a greased large bowl; turn to coat all over with shortening; cover with a towel. Let rise in a warm place, away from drafts, about 1½ hours, or until double in bulk.
6 Punch dough down; knead in bowl a few times. Shape into a ball. Press into a greased 10-cup baking dish. Brush top with soft shortening; sprinkle with cornmeal.
7 Let rise again, in a warm place, away from drafts, 1 hour, or until double in bulk.
8 Bake in a moderate oven (375°) 50 minutes, or until loaf is golden brown, and sounds hollow when tapped. Remove from pan to a wire rack; cool.

Crusty French Loaves

Break off a chunk while warm and slather with butter; makes a "soup and salad" supper a hearty meal

Bake at 400° for 30 minutes.
Makes 3 loaves.

1 envelope active dry yeast
2 cups very warm water
6 cups sifted all-purpose flour
2 tablespoons sugar
3 teaspoons salt
2 tablespoons vegetable shortening
   Cornmeal
1 egg white
1 tablespoon cold water

1 Sprinkle yeast into very warm water in a large bowl. (Very warm water should feel comfortably warm when dropped on wrist.) Stir until the yeast dissolves.
2 Stir in 3 cups of the flour, sugar, salt and shortening; beat until smooth; slowly beat in enough of remaining 3 cups flour to make a stiff dough.
3 Turn out onto a lightly floured surface; knead 5 minutes, or until smooth and elastic, adding only enough extra flour to keep dough from sticking.
4 Place in a greased large bowl; turn to coat all over with shortening; cover with a clean towel. Let rise in a warm place, away from drafts, 45 minutes, or until double in bulk.
5 Punch dough down; cover. Let rise again 30 minutes, or until double in bulk.
6 Punch dough down again; knead 1 minute on a lightly floured surface; divide into 3 even pieces (dough will be sticky). Roll each piece to a 12x9-inch rectangle. Roll up from the short side, jelly roll fashion; tuck ends under.
7 Grease a large cookie sheet; sprinkle with cornmeal. Place loaves, seam-side down, 2 inches apart, on cookie sheet; cover. Let rise again 30 minutes, or until double in bulk.
8 Make several evenly spaced diagonal cuts in top of each loaf. Beat egg white slightly with cold water in a cup; brush over each loaf.
9 Place pan of hot water on bottom shelf in oven; place loaves on shelf above.
10 Bake in hot oven (400°) 30 minutes, or until loaves are golden brown and sound hollow when tapped. Remove from cookie sheet and cool on wire racks.

SPECIAL BREAD TIPS

1 As a simple test for the "very warm" water that's needed to activate the yeast, hold the inside of your wrist under running water. The water should feel comfortably warm when it's just right.

2 For an easy way to determine when dough has doubled in bulk: Press the dough flat in bowl, mark level, then remove dough. Fill bowl with water to double the first mark; mark level.

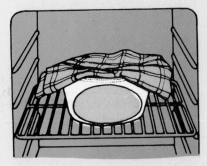

3 For warm, draft-free place to let dough rise, use oven with door closed. If the oven is electric, warm to 200°; then turn off and let cool for 5 minutes. If gas, pilot light will keep dough warm.

WAYS TO SHAPE BREAD

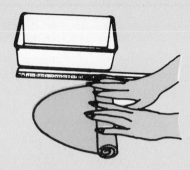

1 To shape a handsome loaf of bread: Roll or pat dough out to a rectangle with short side equal to length of a bread pan. Roll up the dough, in jelly-roll style, pressing the turns firmly.

3 How to smooth ends of loaves: Press the dough down on each end of loaf with sides of hands. Tuck the thin strips formed under the loaf. Lift the loaf to the pan without stretching.

2 When loaf has been shaped, make sure dough is even on both ends. Then, with fingers, pinch long seam firmly—to seal and keep from unrolling. Put in pans, with seam on bottom.

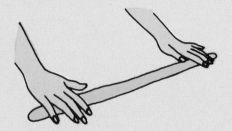

4 For shaping long loaves of bread: Roll up, in jelly-roll style, pinching seam, as in FIG. 2. Then, with the palms of your hands, taper the ends by rolling loaf back and forth on board.

Armenian Bread

It looks like a flying saucer and is the perfect bread to serve at your next barbecue

Bake at 350° for 30 minutes.
Makes three 15- ounce rounds

    2 envelopes active dry yeast
2¼ cups very warm water
    ¾ cup nonfat dry milk
    3 tablespoons sugar
    2 teaspoons salt
    3 tablespoons olive or vegetable oil
6½ cups sifted all-purpose flour
    ¼ cup sesame seeds
    1 egg, beaten

1 Sprinkle yeast into very warm water in a large bowl. (Very warm water should feel comfortably warm when dropped on wrist.) Stir until yeast dissolves, then stir in dry milk, sugar, salt and oil.
2 Beat in 2 cups of the flour until smooth. Beat in enough of the remaining flour to make a soft dough.
3 Turn out onto lightly floured pastry board. Knead until smooth and elastic, about 10 minutes, using only as much flour as needed to keep dough from sticking.
4 Invert a large bowl over dough and allow to rest 20 minutes.
5 Divide dough into 4 pieces. Divide one of these pieces into 3 pieces. Grease 3 cooky sheets with oil. Pat out one of the large pieces of dough to a 9-inch round on one of the cooky

sheets. Make a 3-inch hole in center of round by pulling dough back with fingers. Pat a small piece of dough into a 3-inch round and place in center. Repeat to make 3 loaves. Cover each loaf with plastic wrap and chill 2 hours, or to a maximum of 6 hours.
6 Remove breads from refrigerator and remove plastic wrap. Allow to stand at room temperature 10 minutes.
7 Sprinkle sesame seeds on a shallow baking pan. Toast in a moderate oven (350°), 5 minutes, or just until golden.
8 Brush breads with beaten egg and sprinkle with toasted sesame seeds.
9 Bake in moderate oven (350°) 30 minutes, or until breads are golden and give a hollow sound when tapped. Remove from cooky sheets to wire racks; cool completely.

Taos Bread

This Pueblo Indian bread is shaped in the form of the sun to honor the Sun God

Bake at 350.° for 50 minutes.
Makes three 13- ounce loaves.

1½ cups water
3 tablespoons butter or margarine
1 tablespoon sugar
3 teaspoons salt
2 envelopes active dry yeast
½ cup very warm water
6½ cups sifted all-purpose flour

1 Combine water, butter or margarine, sugar and salt in a small saucepan. Heat slowly until butter or margarine melts; cool to lukewarm.
2 Sprinkle yeast into very warm water in a large bowl. (Very warm water should feel comfortably warm when dropped on wrist.) Stir until yeast dissolves, then stir in butter mixture.
3 Beat in 4 cups of flour until smooth. Beat in enough remaining flour to make a soft dough.
4 Turn out onto a lightly floured pastry board; knead until smooth and elastic, about 5 minutes, using only as much flour as needed to keep dough from sticking.
5 Place in a greased large bowl; turn to coat all over with shortening; cover with a clean towel. Let rise in a warm place, away from draft, 1½ hours, or until double in bulk.
6 Punch dough down; turn out onto board; knead a few times; divide dough into 3 equal pieces. Shape each piece into a ball. Cover with a towel, let rest 10 minutes.
7 On the pastry board, roll each ball into a

9-inch circle. Fold each circle almost in half. Top circular edge should be about 1 inch from bottom circular edge. Place on greased cooky sheet. With kitchen scissors, make about 6 gashes in the dough, cutting from the circular edge about ⅔ the way inward to the folded edge. Spread the fingers of dough apart so they will not touch each other while baking. Do the same with the remaining 2 balls of dough. Let rise again in warm place, away from draft, 1 hour, or until double in bulk.
8 Bake in moderate oven (350°) 50 minutes, or until breads are golden, and give a hollow sound when tapped. Remove from cooky sheet to wire racks; cool completely.

SHARP AND SWEET CHEESE BREADS

Anadama Cheese Bread

Perk up this old New England favorite with cheese and a bubble top

Bake at 375° for 35 minutes.
Makes two 28- ounce loaves

1½ cups water
½ cup corn meal
2 teaspoons salt
¼ cup vegetable shortening
½ cup light molasses
2 envelopes active dry yeast
½ cup very warm water
6 cups sifted all-purpose flour
8 ounces process American cheese, shredded (2 cups)
Butter or margarine, melted
Corn meal (for topping)

1 Combine 1½ cups water, ½ cup corn meal, salt, shortening and molasses in a medium-size saucepan. Heat, stirring constantly, until thick and bubbly. Pour into a large bowl; cool until lukewarm.
2 Sprinkle yeast into the ½ cup very warm water in a small bowl. (Very warm water should feel comfortably warm when dropped on wrist.) Stir until yeast dissolves; stir into corn meal mixture.
3 Beat in 2 cups of flour until smooth; stir in cheese, then about 3 more cups of the flour, one at a time, until mixture forms a soft dough.

(continued)

4 Turn dough out onto lightly floured pastry board. Knead until smooth and elastic, about 8 minutes, using only as much flour as needed to keep dough from sticking.

5 Place in a greased large bowl; turn to coat all over with shortening; cover with a clean towel. Let rise in a warm place, away from draft, 45 minutes, or until double in bulk.

6 Punch dough down; knead a few times. Divide dough in half, then divide one half into 14 even-size balls, rolling each ball between palms of floured hands until surface is smooth. Place a row of 5 balls along each long side of a 9x5x3-inch greased loaf pan; place a row of 4 balls down the center. Repeat with remaining half of dough in a second loaf pan.

7 Brush tops of loaves with melted butter or margarine and sprinkle lightly with corn meal. Let rise in a warm place, away from draft, 30 minutes, or until double in bulk.

8 Bake in moderate oven (375°) 35 minutes, or until loaves give a hollow sound when tapped. Remove from pans to wire racks; cool completely. Loaves will break into separate rolls for serving.

Swiss Batter Bread

Each slice of this loaf tastes teasingly of cheese

Bake at 350° for 1 hour and 10 minutes.
Makes 1 large loaf.

⅔ cup water
2 tablespoons sugar
3 teaspoons salt
1 tablespoon butter or margarine
1 small can evaporated milk (⅔ cup)
2 packages active dry yeast or 2 cakes compressed yeast
⅔ cup very warm water
4½ cups sifted all-purpose flour
2 cups grated Swiss cheese (8 ounces)

1 Heat the ⅔ cup water with sugar, salt and butter or margarine just to boiling in a small saucepan; stir into evaporated milk in a small bowl; cool to lukewarm.

2 Sprinkle or crumble yeast into very warm water in a large bowl. (Very warm water should feel comfortably warm when dropped on wrist.) Stir until yeast dissolves, then stir in cooled milk.

3 Beat in 2 cups of the flour until almost smooth. Stir in cheese and remaining flour until well-blended, then beat vigorously with a spoon, scraping down side of bowl often, 20 strokes, or until dough is very stiff.

There's plenty of variety in this selection of tasty breads (check index for recipes): **Vienna Crescent** (from top) **Anadama Cheese Bread, Parmesan Garlic Bread,** and **Taos Bread.**

4 Cover with a clean towel; let rise in a warm place, away from drafts, 45 minutes, or until the dough is double in bulk.

5 Stir dough down; beat again about 10 strokes; spoon into a greased 8-cup (2-quart) round baking dish. Cover; let rise again, 30 minutes, or until not quite double in bulk.

6 Bake in lower ⅓ of moderate oven (350°) 1 hour and 10 minutes, or until bread gives a hollow sound when tapped. (If bread starts to get too brown, cover it lightly with foil during last 30 minutes of baking.) Remove from dish; cool.

Cheese Bread

Each slice of this mellow moist bread tastes teasingly of snappy Cheddar

Bake at 350° for 45 minutes for medium-size loaves, 30 minutes for miniature ones.
Makes 4 medium-size loaves,
or 2 medium-size and 6 miniature loaves,
or 12 miniature loaves

1 cup milk
2 tablespoons sugar
3 teaspoons salt
1 tablespoon butter or margarine
1 envelope active dry yeast
1 cup very warm water
5 cups sifted all-purpose flour
2 cups grated sharp Cheddar cheese (8 ounces)

1 Scald milk with sugar, salt, and butter or margarine in a small saucepan; cool to lukewarm.

2 Sprinkle yeast into very warm water in a large bowl. (Very warm water should feel comfortably warm when dropped on wrist.) Stir until yeast dissolves, then stir in cooled milk mixture.

3 Beat in 1 cup of the flour; sprinkle cheese over and beat in until completely blended. Beat in remaining 4 cups flour gradually to make a stiff dough.

4 Turn out onto a lightly floured pastry cloth or board; knead until smooth and elastic, adding

(continued)

only enough extra flour to keep dough from sticking.

5 Place in a greased bowl; turn to coat all over with shortening; cover with a clean towel. Let rise in warm place, away from draft, 1 hour, or until double in bulk.

6 Punch dough down; knead a few times, then shape this way: If making all medium-size loaves, divide dough in quarters; shape each into a loaf. If making medium-size and miniature loaves, divide dough in half; shape one half into 2 loaves, then divide remaining half into sixths; shape each into a loaf. If making all miniature loaves, divide all the dough in twelfths; shape each into a loaf. Place medium-size loaves in greased pans, 7½x3¾x2¼; miniature ones in greased toy-size loaf pans; cover. Let rise again in warm place, away from draft, about 1 hour, or until double in bulk.

7 Bake in moderate oven (350°) 45 minutes for medium-size loaves, 30 minutes for miniature ones, or until bread gives a hollow sound when tapped. Remove from pans; brush tops with more butter or margarine; cool on wire racks.

Wrapping tip: Cool bread completely, then wrap in transparent wrap. (Bread is likely to steam if wrapped warm.)

Parmesan Garlic Bread

Brush pans with garlic butter to give just a tease of garlic flavor to the bread

Bake at 400° for 40 minutes for large loaves, 30 to 35 minutes for small.
Makes two 2-pound loaves, or 8 medium-size loaves, or 14 miniature-size loaves

  2 cups milk
  2 tablespoons sugar
  2 teaspoons salt
  2 envelopes active dry yeast
  2 cups very warm water
10 cups sifted all-purpose flour
  1 cup grated Parmesan cheese
  1 clove garlic, crushed
  2 tablespoons butter or margarine, melted
    Grated Parmesan cheese

1 Heat milk with sugar and salt in small sauce pan just to lukewarm.

2 Sprinkle yeast into very warm water in a large bowl. (Very warm water should feel comfortably warm when dropped on wrist.) Stir until yeast dissolves, then stir in cooled milk mixture.

3 Beat in 5 cups flour and 1 cup cheese until completely blended. Beat in remaining flour gradually to make a soft dough.

4 Turn out onto lightly floured pastry board; knead until smooth and elastic, adding only enough extra flour to keep dough from sticking.

5 Place in greased large bowl; turn to coat all over with shortening; cover with a clean towel. Let rise in warm place, away from draft, 1 hour, or until double in bulk. Stir garlic into butter. Brush pans or casseroles with garlic butter.

6 Punch dough down; knead 1 minute on lightly floured pastry board, then shape this way: For large loaves, divide dough in half, divide each half in 7 even pieces, shape into rolls; place 6 rolls around edge of prepared pan and 1 in center. For medium-size loaves: Divide dough into 16 even pieces; shape into rolls, place 2 rolls in each of 8 prepared ten-ounce casseroles or custard cups. For miniature loaves: Divide dough into 14 pieces, shape into loaves, place in prepared toy-size loaf pans; cover. Let rise again in warm place, away from draft, 45 minutes, or until double in bulk. Brush tops with water; sprinkle lightly with extra Parmesan cheese.

7 Bake in very hot oven (400°) 40 minutes for large loaves, 30 to 40 minutes for small and medium loaves, or until breads give a hollow sound when tapped. Remove from pans to wire racks; cool completely.

Little Dill Cheese Loaves

Cottage cheese enhances the flavor of this simple-to-make batter bread

Bake at 350° for 45 minutes.
Makes 6 individual loaves

  1 package active dry yeast
 ½ cup very warm water
  1 cup (½ pound) cream-style cottage cheese
  2 tablespoons sugar
  1 tablespoon instant minced onion
  2 teaspoons dill weed
  1 teaspoon salt
 ¼ teaspoon baking soda
  1 egg
2⅓ cups sifted all-purpose flour
    Butter or margarine

1 Sprinkle yeast into very warm water in a large bowl. (Very warm water should feel comfortably warm when dropped on wrist.) Stir until yeast dissolves.

2 Heat cheese just until lukewarm in small saucepan; stir into yeast mixture; add sugar, onion, dill weed, salt, baking soda, egg and 1⅓ cups flour. Beat with electric mixer at medium speed for 2 minutes. Stir in the remaining flour to make a soft dough.

3 Cover with a clean towel. Let rise in a warm place, away from draft, 1 hour, or until double in bulk.

4 Stir dough down; spoon evenly into six 6-ounce soufflé dishes or custard cups.

5 Let rise again in warm place, away from draft, 45 minutes, or until double in bulk.

6 Bake in moderate oven (350°) 30 minutes; cover with foil, then bake 15 minutes longer, or until loaves give a hollow sound when tapped. Brush tops with butter or margarine; remove from dishes to wire racks. Serve warm or cool completely.

FANCIFUL TWISTS

Two-Tone Rye Twist

Light and dark rye, twisted together, start from the same basic dough.

Bake at 350° for 45 minutes.
Makes two 20- ounce loaves

4 cups sifted all-purpose flour
4 cups whole-rye flour
2 envelopes active dry yeast
2½ cups very warm water
¼ cup (½ stick) butter or margarine, melted
⅓ cup dark molasses
3 teaspoons salt
2 teaspoons caraway seeds, crushed
1 cup whole-bran cereal
¼ cup dry cocoa (not a mix)
2 teaspoons instant coffee
Corn meal
Butter or margarine, melted

1 teaspoon cornstarch
½ cup cold water

1 Combine 3 cups all-purpose flour with rye flour in a medium-size bowl; blend well; reserve.

2 Sprinkle yeast into very warm water in a large bowl. (Very warm water should feel comfortably warm when dropped on wrist.) Stir until yeast dissolves; stir in butter or margarine, molasses, salt and caraway. Pour one half of mixture into a second large bowl.

3 To one half of the yeast mixture, add the bran, cocoa and coffee, stirring to mix well. Stir in enough of the rye-flour mixture to make a soft dough (about 3 cups). Turn dough out onto a lightly floured pastry board. Knead until smooth and elastic, about 5 minutes, using only as much of the remaining all-purpose flour as needed to keep dough from sticking.

4 Place dough in a greased medium-size bowl; turn to coat all over with shortening; cover with clean towel. Let rise in a warm place, away from draft, 45 minutes, or until double in bulk.

5 To remaining half of yeast mixture, stir in enough rye-flour mixture, part at a time, to make a soft dough (about 3½ cups). Turn out onto lightly floured board. Knead until smooth and elastic about 5 minutes, adding only as much of the remaining all-purpose flour as needed to keep dough from sticking. Let rise as in Step 4.

6 Grease two large cooky sheets; sprinkle with cornmeal.

7 When both doughs have doubled, punch down; knead each a few times; divide each in half. Roll each of the four pieces on board with hands to form a thick rope 18 inches long. For each loaf: Twist light and dark rope together; pinch together at ends. Place loaf on cooky sheet; repeat with remaining 2 ropes.

8 Let rise again in a warm place away from draft, 45 minutes, or until double in bulk. Brush lightly with melted butter or margarine.

9 Bake in moderate oven (350°) 45 minutes, or until loaves give a hollow sound when tapped.

10 While loaves are baking, combine cornstarch with cold water in small saucepan, stir until smooth. Cook, stirring constantly, until mixture thickens and boils 1 minute. Brush over baked loaves; return to oven; bake another 3 minutes. Remove from cooky sheets to wire racks; cool completely.

Almond Sugar Twist

Popular in Denmark, this sweet bread has an almond filling, a nut-sugar topping

Bake at 375° for 30 minutes.
Makes 1 large round loaf

¼ cup milk
½ cup (1 stick) butter or margarine
½ cup sugar
½ teaspoon salt
1 envelope active dry yeast
¼ cup very warm water
2 eggs
3 cups sifted all-purpose flour
½ cup almond paste
3 tablespoons cold water
¼ cup sliced almonds

1 Scald milk in a small saucepan; stir in ¼ cup of the butter or margarine, ¼ cup of the sugar, and salt; cool to lukewarm.
2 Sprinkle yeast into very warm water in a large bowl. (Very warm water should feel comfortably warm when dropped on wrist.) Stir until yeast dissolves, then stir in cooled milk mixture.
3 Beat eggs in a small bowl; save 1 table-spoonful for Step 7; beat remaining into yeast mixture. stir in 2 cups of the flour until smooth; beat vigorously 100 strokes, then beat in remaining flour.
4 Place in a greased large bowl; cover with a clean towel. Let rise in a warm place, away from draft, 1¼ hours, or until double in bulk.
5 Mix almond paste with remaining ¼ cup butter or margarine, 3 tablespoons of remaining sugar, and 2 tablespoons of the cold water.
6 Punch dough down; knead until smooth and elastic on a lightly floured pastry cloth or board. Roll out to a rectangle, 20x10; spread with almond filling almost to edges. Starting at one long side, roll up, jelly-roll fashion. Place one end in the center of a greased large cooky sheet, then coil roll loosely round and round to make a "snail;" tuck end under. Cover; let rise again 30 minutes, or until double in bulk.
7 Stir remaining 1 tablespoon water into saved beaten egg; brush over "snail;" sprinkle with sliced almonds and remaining 1 tablespoon sugar.
8 Bake in moderate oven (375°) 30 minutes, or until golden and loaf gives a hollow sound when tapped. Remove from cooky sheet; cool on a wire rack. Serve warm or cold.

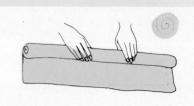

ALMOND SUGAR TWIST

Rolling dough, jelly-roll style, then winding, round and round, are the only tricks needed here. When making the coil, it's easy to handle if you place one end of roll on cooky sheet, then start winding.

Sesame Twist

Light and puffy with toasted sesame seeds all over

Bake at 375° for 45 minutes.
Makes 1 large loaf.

1¼ cups milk
3 tablespoons honey
2 tablespoons shortening
2 teaspoons salt
1 envelope active dry yeast
¼ cup very warm water
4 cups sifted all-purpose flour
1 egg, slightly beaten
1 tablespoon sesame seeds

1 Scald milk with honey, shortening, and salt in a small saucepan; cool to lukewarm.
2 Sprinkle yeast into very warm water in a large bowl. (Very warm water should feel comfortably warm when dropped on wrist.) Stir until yeast dissolves, then stir in cooled milk mixture.
3 Beat in 2 cups of the flour to form a smooth soft dough. Gradually beat in remaining 2 cups flour to make a stiff dough.
4 Turn out onto a lightly floured pastry cloth or board; knead until smooth and elastic, adding only enough extra flour to keep dough from sticking.
5 Place in a greased large bowl; turn to coat all over with shortening; cover with a clean towel. Let rise in a warm place, away from draft, 1½ hours, or until double in bulk.
6 Punch dough down; knead a few times; divide in half. Divide one half into 3 equal-size pieces; roll each into a rope, 14 inches long.

Braid ropes, pinching at ends to hold in place; place braid diagonally on a greased large cooky sheet or in a jelly-roll pan, 15x10x1.

7 Cut off one third of the second half of dough and set aside for next step. Divide remaining into 3 equal-size pieces; roll each into a rope, 12 inches long, and braid, following Step 6; place on top of large braid on cooky sheet.

8 Repeat dividing into thirds, rolling, and braiding with remaining dough, making a braid about 10 inches long; place on top of other two braids; cover. Let rise again in a warm place, away from draft, 1 hour, or until double in bulk.

9 Brush loaf all over with slightly beaten egg; sprinkle with sesame seeds.

10 Bake in moderate oven (375°) 45 minutes, or until golden and loaf gives a hollow sound when tapped. (If loaf starts to get too brown after about 20 minutes' baking, cover top loosely with foil.) Remove from cooky sheet; cool on a wire rack.

Glazed Cinnamon Twist

When you are in a creative mood, make this coffee go-along

Bake at 350° F. 20 to 25 minutes.
Makes 1 braid.

½ DANISH PASTRY DOUGH I *(see index)*
½ *cup melted butter or margarine (1 stick)*
½ *cup sugar*
2 *teaspoons cinnamon*
½ *cup sifted (10X confectioners' powdered) sugar*
1½ *teaspoons water*

1 Roll ⅓ *Basic Sweet Dough* into rectangle, 10x16; spread with butter or margarine; sprinkle with sugar and cinnamon; fold one long side to center; fold other long side over, forming 3 layers; seal edges; place on buttered cooky sheet.

2 Cut lengthwise through middle to within 1 inch of one end; twist strips around each other to form braids; seal ends.

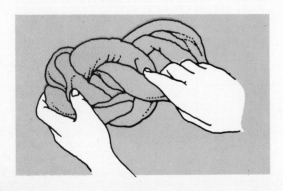

3 Make oval with braid; join ends; press firmly to seal; turn half of oval over to make a figure 8.

4 Cover; let rise in warm place, away from draft, about 30 minutes, or until double in bulk.

5 Bake in moderate oven (350° F.) 20 to 25 minutes, or until golden-brown; place on wire cake rack.

6 Blend 10X sugar and water; drizzle over warm braid.

Date-Nut Ring

One of the most popular twists—and also one of the easiest to make

Bake at 350° F. 20 to 25 minutes.
Makes 1 ring.

½ DANISH PASTRY DOUGH I *(see index)*
1 *package (6½ ounces) pitted dates*
½ *cup sugar*
½ *cup water*
½ *cup chopped walnuts*
¼ *cup melted butter or margarine (½ stick)*
    Sifted 10X (confectioners' powdered) sugar

1 While *Basic Sweet Dough* rises, combine dates, sugar, and water; bring to boiling; simmer 10 minutes, stirring constantly; remove from heat; stir in nuts; cool.

2 Roll ⅓ dough into rectangle, 10x16; spread with butter or margarine and date-nut mixture; fold one long side to center; fold other long side over, forming 3 layers; seal edges; place on buttered cooky sheet.

3 Cut lengthwise through middle to within 1

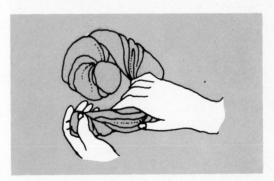

inch of one end; twist strips around each other to form braid; seal ends.

4 Starting with uncut end, wind braid around itself; tuck outer end under edge; press firmly to seal.

(continued)

5 Cover; let rise in warm place, away from draft, about 30 minutes, or until double in bulk.
6 Bake in moderate oven (350° F.) 20 to 25 minutes, or until golden-brown; cool on cake rack; sift 10X sugar over top.

Lemon Twist

Friends and family will enjoy this lemon and walnut twist

> Bake at 350° F. 20 to 25 minutes.
> Makes 1 braid.

¾ cup sugar
1 tablespoon grated lemon rind
½ cup chopped walnuts
½ DANISH PASTRY DOUGH I *(see index)*
¼ cup melted butter or margarine (½ stick)
  Walnut halves

1 Combine sugar, rind, and nuts.
2 Roll ⅓ *Basic Sweet Dough* into rectangle, 10x16; spread with melted butter or margarine and sugar-nut mixture. Starting at long side of dough, roll up, jelly-roll fashion; press edge to seal; place on buttered cooky sheet.

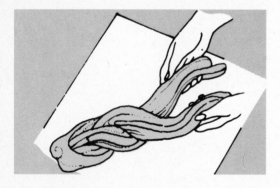

3 Cut lengthwise through middle to within 1 inch of one end; turn strips cut side up; twist strips around each other, keeping cut sides up, to form braid; seal ends.
4 Cover; let rise in warm place, away from draft, about 30 minutes, or until double in bulk; garnish with walnut halves.
5 Bake in moderate oven (350° F.) 20 to 25 minutes, or until golden-brown; place on wire cake rack to cool.

SUCCULENT FRUIT BREADS

Candied Fruit Loaf

A dessert loaf the whole family can enjoy

> Bake at 350° for 35 minutes.
> Makes 2 large coffee cakes.

5½ cups sifted all-purpose flour
2 envelopes active dry yeast
⅓ cup sugar (for dough)
2 teaspoons salt
¾ cup (1½ sticks) butter or margarine
1 cup water
½ cup milk
1 teaspoon vanilla
2 eggs
¾ cup wheat germ
1 cup mixed candied fruits, chopped
2 tablespoons sugar (for filling)
½ cup finely chopped blanched almonds

1 Mix 2 cups of the flour, undissolved yeast, the ⅓ cup sugar, and salt in a large bowl; add ½ cup of the butter or margarine.
2 Heat water and milk until very warm to the touch (not scalding) in a small saucepan; add to flour mixture with vanilla. Beat with electric mixer at medium speed 2 minutes.
3 Beat eggs slightly in a small bowl; measure out 2 tablespoonfuls and set aside for glaze. Add remaining eggs and 1 cup more flour to yeast mixture; beat with electric mixer at high speed 1 minute, or until dough is thick and elastic. Stir in ½ cup of the wheat germ, candied fruits, and remaining flour to make a soft dough.
4 Turn out onto a lightly floured pastry cloth or board; knead until smooth and elastic, adding only enough extra flour to keep dough from sticking. Cover with transparent wrap; let stand 20 minutes.
5 Combine the 2 tablespoons sugar and remaining ¼ cup wheat germ in a small bowl; cut in remaining ¼ cup butter or margarine until mixture is crumbly; stir in almonds.
6 Divide dough in half; roll, half at a time, to a 12-inch square. Sprinkle half of the almond mixture over top; press in lightly; roll up, jelly-roll fashion. Place, seam side down, on a lightly greased cooky sheet. Repeat with second half of dough.
7 Make cuts, 1½ inches apart, along one side of roll from outer edge to center. Repeat on other side, spacing cuts halfway between those

Bake your Holiday presents. These two breads, **Polka-Dot Raisin Log** (front) and **Candied Fruit Loaf** (behind) are perfect for gift-giving.

on opposite side. Turn each slice slightly on its side. Cover loosely with transparent wrap; chill 2 hours.

8 Remove from refrigerator; uncover; let stand 10 minutes. Stir 1 tablespoon water into remaining beaten egg; brush over coffee cakes.

9 Bake in moderate oven (350°) 35 minutes, or until golden and coffee cakes give a hollow sound when tapped. Remove from cooky sheets to wire racks; cool slightly. Garnish with small wedges of green and yellow candied pineapple, if you wish. Slice crosswise; serve warm or cold.

Currant Batter Bread

Mix this one up quickly; you'll have a fragrant warm loaf ready to enjoy in almost no time at all

Bake at 350° for 40 minutes.
Makes 1 loaf.

¾ cup milk
6 tablespoons sugar
1 teaspoon salt
5 tablespoons butter or margarine
1 teaspoon grated orange rind
¼ cup very warm water
1 envelope active dry yeast
3 eggs, beaten
3 cups sifted all-purpose flour
1 cup dried currants
½ cup 10X (confectioners') sugar
1 tablespoon orange juice

1 Heat milk, sugar, salt and butter or margarine in a small saucepan, just until butter is melted. Cool milk mixture to lukewarm. Stir in orange rind.

2 Measure very warm water into a large bowl; sprinkle in yeast. (Very warm water should feel comfortably warm when dropped on wrist.) Stir until dissolved. Add lukewarm milk mixture and eggs. Blend in flour, 1 cup at a time. Beat until smooth. Stir in currants. Turn into greased 6-cup (1½-quart) baking dish.

3 Cover; let rise 45 minutes, or until double in bulk.

4 Bake in a moderate oven (350°) 40 minutes, or until loaf is golden brown and sounds hollow when tapped.

5 Cool a few minutes on wire rack; remove bread from baking dish. Blend 10X sugar and orange juice in a cup. While bread is still warm, drizzle with glaze.

Christmastime in Italy is **Panettone,** a fruit-studded bread with a sweet and soft dough. Surprise your family this Yuletime with this easy-to-make and delectable bread.

Panettone

A traditional sweet fruit-filled bread from Italy. Delicious plain or toasted.

Bake at 375° for 1 hour and 15 minutes.
Makes 1 large round loaf

½ cup milk
2 teaspoons anise seeds
½ cup sugar
1 teaspoon salt
1 envelope active dry yeast
¼ cup very warm water
2 eggs, beaten

2 teaspoons grated lemon rind
3 cups sifted all-purpose flour
½ cup (1 stick) butter or margarine, melted and cooled
1 jar (8 ounces) mixed candied fruits (1 cup), chopped fine
½ cup seedless raisins

1 Scald milk with anise seeds in small saucepan; remove from heat. Let stand 5 minutes, then strain into a cup, discarding seeds. Stir in ¼ cup sugar and salt. (Save remaining ¼ cup sugar for Step 6.) Cool just until warm.
2 Sprinkle yeast into very warm water in large bowl. (Very warm water should feel comfortably

warm when dropped on wrist.) Stir until dissolved.

3 Stir in cooled milk mixture, eggs, lemon rind, and flour. Beat vigorously, scraping down side of bowl. Continue to beat with a spoon 100 times, or until dough is elastic and forms a ball. (This will take about 5 minutes.) Stir in cooled melted butter or margarine. Dough will become stringy, so beat again until it forms a ball.

4 Place in greased bowl; cover with clean towel. Let rise in warm place, away from draft, 1 hour, or until double in bulk.

5 While dough rises, prepare a 6-inch spring-form pan or 6-cup straight-side baking dish this way: Cut a piece of foil, long enough to wrap around pan and overlap slightly; fold in quarters lengthwise. Grease pan and foil strip, then wrap strip around top of pan to make a 2-inch stand-up collar; hold in place with paper clip and string.

6 Sprinkle saved ¼ cup sugar over raised dough; stir down; work in candied fruits and raisins. Place in pan.

7 Cover with clean towel; let rise in warm place, away from draft, 1½ hours, or until double in bulk.

8 Bake in moderate oven (375°) 1 hour and 15 minutes, or until a deep rich brown and loaf gives a hollow sound when tapped. Cool 5 minutes on wire rack. Remove foil collar, then remove bread from pan. Cool completely.

Coffee Crown Cake

"Luscious" is the word for this handsome loaf, delicately flavored with orange and spice

Bake at 350° for 30 minutes.
Makes 1 nine-inch crown

¾ cup milk
⅓ cup sugar
2 packages active dry yeast
½ cup very warm water
2 eggs, beaten
4 cups biscuit mix
1 teaspoon ground cardamom
½ cup (4-ounce jar) candied orange peel
½ cup golden raisins
SYRUP GLAZE (see index for Carioca Pinwheel Loaf)
½ cup 10X (confectioners' powdered) sugar
1 tablespoon water

1 Scald milk in small saucepan; stir in sugar; cool to lukewarm.
2 Dissolve yeast in very warm water in large bowl. (Very warm water should feel comfortably

warm when dropped on wrist.) Stir in cooled milk mixture and beaten eggs.

3 Beat in 2 cups biscuit mix and cardamom until smooth. Stir in orange peel and raisins, saving about 1 tablespoonful of each for decorating top, in Step 8. Beat in remaining biscuit mix to make a soft dough; then beat about 100 strokes to make bread high and light when baked.

4 Cover bowl with clean towel; let rise in warm place, away from draft, 1 hour, or until double in bulk.

5 Punch dough down; beat another 100 strokes; pour into well-greased 10-cup tube mold or 9-inch tube pan.

6 Cover with clean towel; let rise again in warm place, away from draft, 1 hour, or until double in bulk.

7 Bake in moderate oven (350°) 30 minutes, or until golden-brown. Cool in pan on wire rack 10 minutes; turn upside down and remove from pan. Brush with SYRUP GLAZE; let stand until cool.

8 Blend 10X sugar and water in cup; drizzle over crown; decorate with saved orange peel and raisins.

Stollen

This traditional European fruit loaf looks like a giant Parker House roll

Bake at 350° for 35 minutes.
Makes 2 large loaves

1 cup seedless raisins
1 cup (8-ounce jar) mixed chopped candied fruits
¼ cup orange juice
¾ cup milk
½ cup sugar
1 teaspoon salt
1 cup (2 sticks) butter or margarine
2 envelopes active dry yeast
¼ cup very warm water
2 eggs, beaten
1 teaspoon grated lemon rind
5 cups sifted all-purpose flour
1 cup chopped blanched almonds
¼ teaspoon nutmeg
2 tablespoons cinnamon-sugar

1 Combine raisins, candied fruits, and orange juice in a small bowl.
2 Scald milk with sugar, salt, and ½ cup (1 stick)

(continued)

of the butter or margarine; cool to lukewarm. Sprinkle yeast into very warm water in a large bowl. (Very warm water should feel comfortably warm when dropped on wrist.) Stir until yeast dissolves, then stir in cooled milk mixture, eggs, and lemon rind.

3 Beat in 2 cups of the flour until smooth; stir in fruit mixture, almonds, and nutmeg, then beat in just enough of remaining 3 cups flour to make a stiff dough. Knead until smooth and elastic on a lightly floured pastry cloth or board, adding only enough flour to keep dough from sticking.

4 Place in a greased large bowl; cover with a clean towel. Let rise in a warm place, away from draft, 2 hours, or until double in bulk.

5 Punch dough down; knead a few times; divide in half. Roll each into an oval, 15x9; place on a greased large cooky sheet. Melt remaining ½ cup (1 stick) butter or margarine in a small saucepan; brush part over each oval; sprinkle with cinnamon-sugar; fold in half lengthwise. Cover; let rise again 1 hour, or until double in bulk. Brush again with part of the remaining melted butter or margarine.

6 Bake in moderate oven (350°) 35 minutes, or until golden and loaves give a hollow sound when tapped. While hot, brush with remaining melted butter or margarine; cool on wire racks.

STOLLEN

This homey loaf starts with a big oval of dough folded over to resemble a jumbo Parker House roll.

Christmas Stollen

Lemon-scented, buttery, fruit-filled coffee cake that deserves its place as the No. 1 favorite at Christmas

Bake at 375° for 30 minutes.
Makes 2 loaves.

1 envelope active dry yeast
¼ cup very warm water
½ cup sugar

¾ cup milk
½ teaspoon salt
¾ cup (1½ sticks) butter or margarine
1 teaspoon almond extract
1 tablespoon grated lemon rind
2 eggs
5 to 5½ cups sifted all-purpose flour
1 cup mixed candied fruits, chopped
1 cup raisins
½ cup citron, chopped
½ cup candied red cherries
½ cup almonds, chopped
   10X (confectioners') sugar

1 Sprinkle yeast into very warm water in a 1-cup measure. (Very warm water should feel comfortably warm when dropped on wrist.) Mix in ¼ teaspoon of the sugar. Stir until yeast dissolves. Let stand until bubbly and double in volume, about 10 minutes.

2 Heat milk with remaining sugar, salt and 10 tablespoons of the butter or margarine in a small saucepan until lukewarm; combine with yeast mixture in a large bowl.

3 Stir in almond extract, lemon rind and eggs. Beat in enough flour to make a soft dough; turn out onto lightly floured surface. Knead until smooth and elastic, about 10 minutes, using enough of remaining flour to keep dough from sticking.

4 Place in a buttered bowl; turn to bring buttered side up. Cover with a towel. Let rise in a warm place, away from drafts, 1 hour, or until double in bulk.

5 Punch dough down; turn out onto lightly floured surface; knead a few times. Invert bowl over dough; let rest 10 minutes. Knead candied fruits, raisins, citron, cherries and almonds into dough until evenly distributed. Divide in half; roll each to a 12x8-inch oval; fold in half by bringing one side of oval over to within ½ inch from edge of other side. Place on one large or two small buttered cookie sheets.

6 Let rise again in a warm place, away from drafts, 45 minutes, or until double in bulk.

7 Bake in moderate oven (375°) 20 minutes; brush with remaining butter or margarine. Bake 10 minutes longer, or until loaves are golden brown and sound hollow when tapped. Remove to wire racks; cool completely. Just before serving, sprinkle with 10X sugar. Or, combine ¼ cup 10X sugar with enough water to make a thin glaze; drizzle over tops.

Take the worry out of Easter cooking with this collection of specialty breads: **Old World Easter Bread** (at back). **Walnut Stickies** (both round and square), and gooey and caramely yeast rolls.

Old World Easter Bread

Idea for this towering sweet bread comes from Russia. If you don't have a tall mold, bake it in a deep bowl

Bake at 350° for 40 minutes.
Makes 1 loaf

⅓ cup milk
¼ cup sugar
½ teaspoon salt
4 tablespoons (½ stick) butter or margarine
1 envelope active dry yeast
¼ cup very warm water
1 egg, beaten
2 cups sifted all-purpose flour
¼ cup candied orange peel (from a 4-ounce jar)
¼ cup golden raisins
¼ teaspoon nutmeg
2 tablespoons fine dry bread crumbs
½ cup sifted 10X (confectioners' powdered) sugar
1 tablespoon water
Yellow food coloring

1 Scald milk with sugar, salt, and butter or margarine in small saucepan; cool just until warm.
2 Sprinkle yeast into very warm water in medium-size bowl. (Very warm water should feel comfortably warm when dropped on wrist.) Stir until yeast dissolves, then sitr in cooled milk mixture and egg.
3 Beat in 1 cup of the flour until smooth; stir in orange peel, raisins, and nutmeg; beat in remaining 1 cup flour to make a soft dough. Beat 100 times.
4 Coat top of dough lightly with butter or margarine; cover with clean towel. Let rise in warm place, away from draft, 1 hour, or until double in bulk.
5 Brush a 6-cup tall mold or 6-cup deep bowl with salad oil; sprinkle with bread crumbs. Punch dough down; beat 100 times. Spoon into mold.
6 Cover with clean towel; let rise in warm place, away from draft, 45 minutes, or until double in bulk.
7 Bake in moderate oven (350°) 40 minutes, or until loaf gives a hollow sound when tapped.

(continued)

Cool 5 minutes on wire rack; remove from mold or bowl.

8 Mix 10X sugar and water in a cup to make a thin frosting; drizzle half over loaf, letting it run down side. Blend a drop or two of yellow food coloring into remaining frosting to tint yellow; drizzle over loaf. Decorate top with a few slivered almonds, if you wish.

SWEET COFFEE CAKES, BUNS AND ROLLS

Sweet Yeast Dough

From this sweet and simple recipe, you can make 24 buns; 2 crumb cakes; or 12 buns and one crumb cake

½ cup milk
½ cup sugar
 1 teaspoon salt
⅔ cup vegetable shortening
 2 envelopes active dry yeast
½ cup very warm water
 4 eggs, beaten
4½ cups sifted all-purpose flour

1 Combine milk, sugar, salt and shortening in saucepan. Heat just until shortening is melted; cool to lukewarm.

2 Sprinkle yeast into very warm water in a large bowl. (Very warm water should feel comfortably warm when dropped on wrist.) Add lukewarm milk mixture, eggs and 2 cups of the flour; beat until smooth. Add just enough of remaining flour to make dough soft.

3 Turn out onto lightly floured surface; knead until smooth and elastic, about 5 minutes, using only as much flour as needed to keep dough from sticking.

4 Place in large greased bowl; turn to bring greased side up. Cover. Let rise in warm place, away from drafts, 1 to 1½ hours, or until double in bulk.

5 Punch dough down; knead a few times; let rest 5 minutes. Shape into BUTTERSCOTCH-NUT BUNS, SUGAR BUNS, CRUMB CAKES, CRUMB BUNS or APPLE KUCHEN.

Who could resist this collection of coffee cakes and sweet rolls? No one. Especially after they've tasted the crunchy **Butterscotch-Nut Buns, Sugar Buns,** and **Crumb Cake.**

Sugar Buns

Sugary roll-ups swirled with icing

Bake at 375° for 25 minutes.
Makes 12 buns.

½ recipe SWEET YEAST DOUGH (see index for recipe)
 2 tablespoons butter or margarine, softened
⅓ cup sugar
½ teaspoon ground cinnamon
½ cup raisins
½ cup 10X (confectioners') sugar
 2 teaspoons milk

1 Roll out SWEET YEAST DOUGH to a 15x8-inch rectangle on a lightly floured surface. Spread entire surface of the dough evenly with the softened butter or margarine.

2 Combine sugar, cinnamon and raisins; sprinkle over dough. Roll up, jelly roll fashion, beginning with the long side. Pinch to seal seam. Cut into 12 equal slices. Place cut side up, in a greased 9-inch square pan. Cover. Let rise 1 hour, or until dough is double in bulk.

3 Blend 10X sugar and milk in a small bowl to make a thin icing.

4 Bake in a moderate oven (375°) 25 minutes, or until golden brown. Turn out on wire rack. Turn right side up. While warm, drizzle icing over tops.

Crumb Cake

This yummy crumb-topped cake makes good eating with a mug of steaming coffee

Bake at 375° for 25 minutes.
Makes one 13x9x2-inch cake.

½ recipe SWEET YEAST DOUGH (see index for recipe)
½ cup (1 stick) butter or margarine, softened
⅓ cup firmly packed brown sugar
 1 cup sifted all-purpose flour
¼ teaspoon ground nutmeg
½ teaspoon ground cinnamon

(continued)

1 Press dough evenly into a greased 13x9x2-inch baking pan. Brush top with part of the softened butter or margarine. Let rise in a warm place, away from drafts, 1 hour, or until double in bulk.
2 Combine remaining butter or margarine, brown sugar, flour, nutmeg and cinnamon in a small bowl. Sprinkle over dough.
3 Bake in moderate oven (375°) 25 minutes, or until golden brown. Remove from oven; cool 5 minutes; loosen cake in pan. Remove from pan this way: Press a sheet of foil lightly over top of cake to hold crumbs in place; turn upside down and lift off pan; turn right side up. Remove to wire rack; cool completely. Sprinkle with 10X sugar, if you wish.

Crumb Buns: Cut dough in pan in 16 sections with a sharp knife dipped in melted butter or margarine. Let rise, top with crumbs and bake as in CRUMB CAKE.

Butterscotch-Nut Buns

Tender buns with a buttery-caramel coating; as pretty as they are delicious

Bake at 375° for 25 minutes.
Makes 12 buns.

¾ *cup firmly packed brown sugar*
½ *cup light corn syrup*
¼ *cup (½ stick) butter or margarine*
½ *cup walnut or pecan halves*
½ *recipe* SWEET YEAST DOUGH *(see index for recipe)*
2 *tablespoons butter or margarine, softened*
⅓ *cup granulated sugar*
½ *teaspoon ground cinnamon*
½ *cup raisins*

1 Combine brown sugar, corn syrup and the ¼ cup butter or margarine in a small saucepan; simmer 2 minutes. Pour into a 9x9x2-inch baking pan. Sprinkle with nuts.
2 Roll out SWEET YEAST DOUGH to a 15x8-inch rectangle on a lightly floured surface. Spread entire surface of the dough with the softened butter or margarine.
3 Combine granulated sugar, cinnamon and raisins; sprinkle over dough. Roll up, jelly roll fashion, beginning with the long side. Pinch to

Nothing brings compliments for the cook more than **Apple Kuchen.** Perfect any time, the glazed apples and coffee combine in a dish that will win raves from family and friends.

seal seam. Cut into 12 equal slices. Place cut slices into prepared pan. Cover. Let rise in warm place, away from drafts, 1 hour, or until double in bulk.
4 Bake in moderate oven (375°) 25 minutes, or until golden brown. Turn upside down on plate. Leave pan in place 5 minutes to allow topping to run over buns; lift off pan.
5 To serve: Separate buns with two forks; serve warm with coffee or tea.

Apple Kuchen

Delicious German coffee cake with a moist apple topping, dripped with butter and brown sugar

Bake at 375° for 30 minutes.
Makes one 13x9x2-inch cake.

½ *recipe* SWEET YEAST DOUGH *(see index for recipe)*
3 *medium-size tart cooking apples*
¼ *cup firmly packed light brown sugar*
½ *teaspoon ground cinnamon*
¼ *teaspoon ground cloves*
¼ *teaspoon ground allspice*
¼ *cup (½ stick) butter or margarine*
⅓ *cup apple jelly*

1 Press dough evenly into a greased 13x9x2-inch baking pan. Cover with towel; let rise in a warm place, away from drafts, 30 minutes, or until dough is almost double in bulk.
2 Meanwhile, pare, quarter and core apples; cut into very thin slices. Mix brown sugar, cinnamon, cloves and allspice in a small bowl. Melt butter or margarine in a small saucepan.
3 Arrange apple slices over dough in an overlapping pattern. Sprinkle with sugar mixture; drizzle with butter or margarine.
4 Bake in a moderate oven (375°) 30 minutes, or until a wooden pick inserted in center comes out clean. Remove from oven.
5 Melt apple jelly in a small saucepan. Brush over apples to glaze. Cool kuchen in pan on wire rack at least 30 minutes before cutting. Serve with whole cream or ice cream, if you wish.

Sweet Coffee-Cake Batter

Whip up this basic batter and make 2 coffee cakes—one to freeze; one to serve at breakfast tomorrow!

  2 envelopes active dry yeast
1½ cups very warm water
  1 cup sugar
  ½ teaspoon salt
  ½ cup (¼ stick) butter or margarine, softened
  4 eggs
5¾ cups sifted all-purpose flour

1 Sprinkle yeast into very warm water in a large bowl. (Very warm water should feel comfortably warm when dropped on wrist.) Stir until yeast dissolves, then stir in sugar, salt, butter or margarine, eggs and 2½ cups of the flour. Beat with electric mixer at low speed for ½ minute; then beat 4 minutes at medium speed.
2 Stir in remaining flour until dough is thick and elastic. Cover with towel. Let rise in a warm place, away from drafts, 1½ hours, or until double in bulk.
3 Follow directions for individual coffee cakes for shaping and baking.

Orange Butter Streusel Coffee Cake

The fresh taste of grated orange rind atop a buttery coffee cake: what better way to brighten your morning?

Bake at 350° for 45 minutes.
Makes one 9-inch square.

  Butter or margarine
¼ recipe SWEET COFFEE-CAKE BATTER (see index for recipe)
¼ cup (½ stick) butter or margarine
½ cup sugar
 1 tablespoon grated orange rind

1 Butter a 9x9x2-inch baking pan.
2 Beat SWEET COFFEE-CAKE BATTER 25 strokes; spoon into prepared pan.
3 Cover pan with towel. Let rise in a warm place, away from drafts, 1 hour, or until double in bulk.
4 Make streusel topping: Mix butter or margarine, sugar and orange rind in a small bowl, until crumbs form.
5 Poke little dents in the top of the cake. Sprinkle topping into dents and all over top of cake.
6 Bake in a moderate oven (350°) 45 minutes, or until golden brown. Remove from pan to wire rack; cool.

Enhance the atmosphere of a high tea or a late-night supper snack with this luscious threesome: (left to right) **Pannettone** and **Poteca,** and **Christmas Stollen** (bottom). (See index for recipes.)

Kugelhupf

Use your fanciest 8-cup mold to bake this delightful, almond-covered Bavarian coffee cake

Bake at 350° for 45 minutes.
Makes 1 coffee cake.

 2 tablespoons butter or margarine
½ cup almonds, sliced
½ recipe SWEET COFFEE-CAKE BATTER (see index for recipe)
½ cup golden raisins
  10X (confectioners') sugar

1 Grease an 8-cup fancy tube mold generously with butter or margarine; sprinkle surface evenly with almonds.
2 Beat SWEET COFFEE-CAKE BATTER 25 strokes; stir in raisins. Spoon batter into prepared pan.
3 Cover pan with towel. Let rise in a warm place, away from drafts, 1 hour, or until double in bulk.
4 Bake in moderate oven (350°) 45 minutes, or until golden brown and cake sounds hollow when tapped. Remove from pan to wire rack; cool. Sprinkle with 10X sugar.

Poteca

This tender sour-cream coffee cake from Yugoslavia has a walnut filling that is just out of this world

Bake at 350° for 40 minutes.
Makes 2 coffee cakes.

 1 cup dairy sour cream
¼ cup milk
¾ cup sugar
 1 teaspoon salt
 2 envelopes active dry yeast
 1 teaspoon sugar
½ cup very warm water
 6 cups sifted all-purpose flour
 4 egg yolks
½ cup (1 stick) very soft butter or margarine
  WALNUT FILLING (recipe follows)
  Honey

(continued)

1 Combine sour cream, milk, the ¾ cup sugar and salt in a medium-size saucepan. Heat slowly, stirring constantly, just until mixture begins to bubble and sugar dissolves; pour into a large bowl to cool.

2 Dissolve yeast and 1 teaspoon sugar in very warm water in a small bowl. (Very warm water should feel comfortably warm when dropped on wrist.) Stir until well blended and allow to stand 10 minutes, or until mixture begins to bubble.

3 Stir yeast into cooled sour cream mixture; beat in 3 cups of flour until very smooth. Cover bowl with a clean cloth. Let rise in a warm place, away from drafts, 45 minutes; beat mixture down.

4 Beat egg yolks until well blended in a medium-size bowl; beat in *very soft* butter or margarine until smooth.

5 Beat egg-butter mixture and enough of remaining flour into yeast mixture to make a soft dough. Turn out onto a lightly floured surface and knead 10 minutes, or until dough is smooth and elastic.

6 Place dough in a greased large bowl; turn over to bring greased side up. Cover; let rise in a warm place, away from drafts, 1 hour, or until double in bulk. Punch dough down; knead a few times; let rest 5 minutes.

7 Divide dough in half; roll out one half on a lightly floured surface, to a 26x10-inch rectangle. Spread half the WALNUT FILLING over dough. Roll up jelly roll fashion, starting with the long end. Place, seam side down, in a well-greased 10-inch bundt pan or a 9-inch angel cake tube pan; press ends together to seal.

8 Repeat with remaining dough and filling to make a second cake. Cover pans with a clean towel; let rise in a warm place, away from drafts, 45 minutes, or until almost double in bulk.

9 Bake in a moderate oven (350°) 40 minutes, or until cakes are golden. Cool in pans on wire racks for 15 minutes; loosen around edges of pans; invert onto wire racks to cool.

10 To serve: Brush cakes with honey and garnish with walnut halves and candied red cherries, if you wish.

Walnut Filling

Makes enough for 2 coffee cakes.

1 package (1 pound) shelled walnuts
4 egg whites
¾ cup sugar
1 teaspoon grated lemon rind
Dash of salt

1 Chop walnuts, about 1 cup at a time, until very fine on a wooden board. (It is essential that the nuts be very fine, so that the cake will cut neatly.)

2 Just before the dough is ready to be spread, beat egg whites in a large bowl until foamy white and double in volume; beat in sugar, 1 tablespoon at a time, until meringue forms firm peaks; gradually fold in chopped nuts, lemon rind and salt until mixture is well blended.

Christmas Tree Breads

So super rich and flavorful, you'll want to serve it several times during the holidays

Bake at 375° for 30 minutes.
Makes 2 long loaves.

4½ cups all purpose flour
2 packages active dry yeast
1 cup milk
½ cup water
⅓ cup sugar
¼ cup (½ stick) butter or margarine
2 teaspoons salt
2 egg yolks
NUT FILLING (recipe follows)
Oil

1 Stir together 1½ cups of the flour and yeast in large bowl of electric mixer.

2 Heat milk, water, sugar, butter or margarine and salt over low heat until very warm. (Butter need not be melted.)

3 Add liquid ingredients to flour-yeast mixture; beat at medium speed of electric mixer about 3 minutes. Add egg yolks and 1 cup flour; continue to beat about 2 minutes. Stir in remaining flour to make a moderately soft dough. Turn out onto lightly floured pastry cloth or board; knead until smooth and shiny, about 5 minutes. Cover dough with bowl or pan and let rest 45 minutes in a warm place, away from draft.

4 Divide dough in half. Roll out one half to a triangle 18-inches long and 15 inches at the base. Spread with half the NUT FILLING. Roll up, jelly-roll fashion, starting at one of the long sides to form a cone. Pinch edges to seal seam.

5 Place, seam-side down, on a large greased cookie sheet. Make cuts with scissors from top surface about ⅔ the way through the dough, at one-inch intervals, leaving last 1½ inches uncut at long end to form base of tree.

6 Place dough on a large cookie sheet. Starting at the top (small end) and alternating sides, pull

first piece of dough to the right and turn out; pull next piece of dough to the left and turn out. Continue forming branches, increasing the width of the tree as you proceed down the trunk. Lightly pull branches together, shortening height of the tree. Repeat with second half of dough to make a second tree. Brush with oil. Let rise in warm place, away from draft, 40 minutes, or until double in bulk.
7 Place in preheated oven. Bake for 30 minutes at 375°.

Nut Filling

Makes about 2 cups.

2 cups finely chopped walnuts
⅓ cup sugar
2 tablespoons butter or margarine, melted
2 egg whites

Stir nuts, sugar, and butter or margarine together in a medium-size bowl. Beat egg whites until stiff in a small bowl; fold into nut mixture with a wire whip until well blended.

Sally Lunn

High-rising yeast bread, faintly spiced, plus a sprinkling of confectioners' sugar

Bake at 350° for 45 minutes.
Makes 1 ten-inch round coffeecake

¾ cup milk
⅓ cup granulated sugar
1 teaspoon salt
½ cup (1 stick) butter or margarine
1 envelope active dry yeast
¼ cup very warm water
3 eggs, well-beaten
1 teaspoon grated lemon rind
½ teaspoon ground mace
4 cups sifted all-purpose flour
10X (confectioners' powdered) sugar

1 Scald milk with granulated sugar, salt, and butter or margarine in a small saucepan; cool to lukewarm.
2 Sprinkle yeast into very warm water in a large bowl. (Very warm water should feel comfortably warm when dropped on wrist.) Stir until yeast dissolves; stir in cooled milk mixture, eggs, lemon rind, and mace.
3 Stir in flour until well-blended, then beat vi-

A new way with an old favorite is sure to grab the attention of any coffee cake lover. And none more so than this **Sally Lunn** crowned with berries.

gorously with a wooden spoon, scraping down side of bowl often, 100 strokes, or until dough is shiny elastic; cover with a towel.
4 Let rise in a warm place, away from draft, 1 hour, or until double in bulk.
5 Stir dough down; spoon into a greased 12-cup tube mold or 10-inch angel-cake pan; cover. Let rise again, 1 hour, or until not quite double in bulk.
6 Bake in moderate oven (350°) 45 minutes, or until bread is golden and gives a hollow sound when tapped. Remove from mold; cool on a wire rack. Sprinkle lightly with 10X sugar.

King's Cake

Traditional for the Mardi Gras celebration in New Orleans: the person who gets the bean in his or her portion becomes king or queen for a day or a week (until the next party)

Bake at 375° for 30 minutes.
Makes one 12-inch ring.

½ cup (1 stick) butter or margarine
1 small can (⅔ cup) evaporated milk
½ cup granulated sugar
2 teaspoons salt
5 eggs
2 envelopes active dry yeast
⅓ cup very warm water
1 tablespoon grated lemon rind
1 tablespoon grated orange rind
5½ cups sifted all-purpose flour
1 dry bean
1 cup 10X (confectioners') sugar
2 tablespoons water
   Candied citron slices
   Tiny candy decorettes
   Gold and silver dragees

1 Combine butter or margarine, evaporated milk, granulated sugar and salt in a small saucepan. Heat slowly; melt butter or margarine; cool to lukewarm.
2 Beat 4 of the eggs in a large bowl; stir in milk mixture.
3 Sprinkle yeast into very warm water in a cup. (Very warm water should feel comfortably warm when dropped on wrist.) Stir; dissolve yeast. Add to egg mixture; blend well. Add lemon and orange rinds.
4 Beat in flour, about 1 cup at a time, to make a stiff dough. Turn onto lightly floured surface; knead until smooth and elastic, about 10 minutes, adding only enough flour to keep dough from sticking.
5 Place in a greased large bowl; bring greased side up; cover with a towel. Let rise in a warm place, away from drafts, 1 hour, or until double in bulk.
6 Punch dough down; knead a few times; divide in half. Using palms of hands, roll half into a rope about 20 inches long; lift ends, and, twisting loosely one or two times, place on a greased large cookie sheet in half circle; repeat with second half of dough, pinching ends of ropes together to form a large ring. Lift ring slightly at one side and push the bean about 1 inch into the dough from the bottom. Cover with towel; let rise again in warm place, away from drafts, about 45 minutes, or until double in bulk.

7 While dough rises, beat remaining egg in a small bowl. Brush over dough.
8 Bake in moderate oven (375°) 30 minutes, or until deep golden brown. Slide onto wire rack; cool.
9 Before serving, mix 10X sugar with water in a cup until smooth. Drizzle over ring, then decorate ring with candied citron, decorettes, and dragees.

Kolache

The Czech way with yeast rolls—sweet and shapely, plump with prune filling

Bake at 350° for 15 minutes.
Makes 2 dozen rolls.

½ cup milk
2 envelopes active dry yeast
½ cup very warm water
¾ cup (1½ sticks) butter or margarine
½ cup sugar
1 teaspoon salt
4 egg yolks
4½ cups sifted all-purpose flour
   PRUNE FILLING (recipe follows)
1 egg

1 Heat milk in a small saucepan until lukewarm.
2 Sprinkle yeast into very warm water in a large bowl. (Very warm water should feel comfortably warm when dropped on wrist.) Stir; dissolve yeast.
3 Beat butter or margarine with sugar, salt and egg yolks in large bowl with electric mixer, until light and fluffy. Stir in yeast mixture, cooled milk, and 2 cups of the flour. Beat 5 minutes at medium speed or 300 strokes by hand.
4 Stir in remaining flour to make a very soft dough; cover with a towel. Let rise in a warm place, away from drafts, 1 hour, or until double in bulk.
5 Stir dough down; turn onto lightly floured surface. Knead several minutes, adding only enough flour to keep dough from sticking; divide in half.
6 Roll out one half to a 12x9-inch rectangle; cut into twelve 3-inch squares. Place 1 tablespoon PRUNE FILLING in center of each. To shape each roll, fold one point over filling to cover, then fold opposite point over top; press to seal. (Filling will show at both ends.) Place, 2 inches apart, on a greased large cookie sheet; cover.
7 Cut remaining dough into 12 even pieces;

shape each into a smooth, even ball; place, 2 inches apart, on a second greased cookie sheet; cover.

8 Let all dough rise again 45 minutes, or until double in bulk.

9 Press large hollows in centers of round rolls with fingertips; place a tablespoon of PRUNE FILLING in each. Beat egg with a tablespoon of water. Brush over tops of rolls.

10 Bake all in a moderate oven (350°) 15 minutes, or until golden. Remove from cookie sheets; cool on wire racks.

PRUNE FILLING

Chop 1 package (12 ounces) pitted prunes; combine with 2 cups water and 2 tablespoons sugar in a medium-size saucepan. Cook slowly, stirring constantly, 15 minutes, or until very thick; cool. Stir in 2 teaspoons grated orange rind. Makes 1¾ cups; enough for 2 dozen rolls.

Yule Kugelhupf

German in origin, this rich coffeecake takes its name from the pan it's baked in

Bake at 350° for 50 minutes.
Makes one 10-inch fluted tube cake.

½ cup milk
½ cup (1 stick) butter or margarine
¾ cup sugar
2 teaspoons grated lemon rind
1 envelope active dry yeast
½ cup very warm water
4 cups all purpose flour
4 eggs
1 teaspoon salt
½ cup sliced almonds
½ cup golden raisins

1 Heat milk, butter or margarine, sugar and lemon rind in a small saucepan, just until butter melts. Cool slightly.

2 Dissolve yeast and 1 teaspoon sugar in very warm water in large bowl of electric mixer. (Very warm water should feel comfortably warm when dropped on wrist.) Stir until well blended and allow to stand 10 minutes, or until mixture begins to bubble.

3 Add cooled milk mixture and 2 cups flour to bowl; beat at high speed for 2 minutes; add eggs, one at a time, beating well after each addition; add remaining 2 cups flour and salt; lower speed to medium; beat 5 minutes longer. Cover bowl with plastic wrap.

4 Let rise in a warm place, away from draft,

1½ hours, or until double in bulk; beat dough down and beat in almonds and raisins. Spoon into a well greased 12-cup kugelhupf or fluted tube pan. Cover; let rise in a warm place 45 minutes, or until almost double in bulk.

5 Bake in moderate oven (350°) 50 minutes, or until cake gives a hollow sound when tapped. (Cover top with aluminum foil during last few minutes of baking, if browning too quickly.) Cool in pan on wire rack 5 minutes; loosen around edge and tube of pan; turn onto wire rack; cool completely. Kugelhupf may be wrapped and frozen.

Poinsettia Coffee Cake

You can make one for the family and another for a friend

Bake at 350° for 30 minutes.
Makes 2 long cakes.

4½ cups all purpose flour
2 packages active dry yeast
½ cup milk
½ cup water
⅓ cup sugar
¼ cup (½ stick) butter or margarine
2 teaspoons salt
1 teaspoon ground coriander or cinnamon
2 eggs
Melted butter or margarine
1 container (8 ounces) candied red cherries, chopped
½ cup chopped walnuts
2 tablespoons sugar

1 Stir together 2 cups of the flour and yeast in large bowl of electric mixer.

2 Heat milk, water, the ⅓ cup sugar, ¼ cup butter or margarine, salt and coriander or cinnamon until very warm in small saucepan, stirring to blend.

3 Add liquid ingredients to flour-yeast mixture and beat until smooth, about 2 minutes at medium speed of mixer or 300 strokes by hand. Blend in eggs. Add 1 cup flour and beat 1 minute on medium speed or 150 strokes by hand. Stir in remaining flour and beat vigorously to make a moderately stiff dough.

4 Turn onto lightly floured pastry cloth or board; knead until smooth and shiny, about 5 minutes. Shape into ball and place in a large greased bowl, turning to grease all sides. Cover and let rise in warm place, away from drafts, 1 hour, or until double in bulk.

(continued)

5 Punch dough down; let rest 10 minutes. Divide dough in half. Roll each half to an 8x15-inch rectangle on lightly floured pastry board or cloth. Brush with melted butter or margarine. Combine cherries, nuts and the 2 tablespoons sugar. Sprinkle half the filling on dough. Roll up tightly, beginning at narrow end. Pinch seam to seal. Cut each roll into 8 slices; make 5 diagonal cuts almost through each slice. Arrange slices in two rows on a large greased cookie sheet. Let rise in warm place, away from drafts, about 30 minutes. Repeat with remaining dough.
6 Bake in moderate oven (350°) 30 minutes, or until golden. (Cover with aluminum foil if browning too quickly.) Cool on cookie sheets 15 minutes. Loosen breads with a long sharp knife; cool completely on wire racks. This coffee cake may be wrapped and frozen.

Hot Cross Buns

These are Easter time's favorites of "one-a-penny, two-a-penny" fame

Bake at 350° for 30 minutes.
Makes 2 pans, 16 buns each

2 envelopes active dry yeast
½ cup very warm water

½ cup (1 stick) butter or margarine
⅔ cup evaporated milk
½ cup sugar
1 teaspoon salt
2 eggs
1 cup dried currants
4½ cups sifted all-purpose flour
¼ teaspoon ground cinnamon
¼ teaspoon ground nutmeg
LEMON ICING or SUGAR ICING (recipes follow)

1 Sprinkle yeast into very warm water in large bowl. (Very warm water should feel comfortably warm when dropped on wrist.) Stir until yeast dissolves.
2 Melt butter or margarine in small saucepan; remove from heat. Add evaporated milk, sugar, and salt, stirring until sugar dissolves; stir into yeast mixture.
3 Beat eggs in small bowl; measure 2 tablespoons into a cup and set aside for brushing buns in Step 8. Stir remaining into yeast mixture, then stir in currants.
4 Sift 2 cups of the flour, cinnamon, and nutmeg over yeast mixture; beat until smooth, then stir in just enough of remaining 2½ cups flour to make a soft dough.
5 Turn out onto lightly floured pastry cloth or board; knead until smooth and elastic, adding only enough flour to keep dough from sticking.
6 Place in greased bowl; brush top lightly with

The day has long gone when you could hear "One a penny, two a penny, Hot Cross Buns," but the flavor is still there—as you'll discover with this updated version of **Hot Cross Buns.**

Whatever your religious affiliation, you'll enjoy **Easter-Egg Ring** and the **Walnut Stickies.**

butter or margarine; cover with clean towel. Let rise in warm place, away from draft, 1 hour, or until double in bulk.

7 Punch dough down; turn out onto lightly floured pastry cloth or board; divide in half. Cut each half into 16 equal-size pieces; shape each lightly into a ball. Place each 16 balls in a greased baking pan. 9x9x2.

8 Cover with clean towel; let rise in warm place, away from draft, 45 minutes, or until double in bulk. Brush top of buns lightly with saved egg.

9 Bake in moderate oven (350°) 30 minutes, or until golden brown; remove from pans; cool on wire racks.

10 Drizzle LEMON ICING or SUGAR ICING from tip of teaspoon on top of buns to make cross.

LEMON ICING
Blend 1 cup unsifted 10X (confectioners' powdered) sugar with 4 teaspoons milk, ¼ teaspoon vanilla, and ¼ teaspoon lemon extract until smooth in small bowl. Makes about ½ cup.

SUGAR ICING
Blend 1 cup unsifted 10X (confectioners') sugar with 2 tablespoons milk and ¼ teaspoon vanilla until smooth in small bowl. Makes about ½ cup.

Easter-Egg Ring

A delightful hot bread for Easter breakfast: the eggs hard-cook while the bread bakes

Bake at 375° for 30 minutes.
Makes 1 sixteen-inch ring.

½ cup milk
2 tablespoons butter or margarine
¼ cup sugar
1 teaspoon salt
1 package active dry yeast
¼ cup very warm water
1 egg, beaten
3 cups sifted all-purpose flour
3 drops oil of anise
6 uncooked white-shell eggs
   Easter-egg coloring
   Butter or margarine

1 Scald milk with 2 tablespoons butter or margarine in small saucepan; stir in sugar and salt; cool to lukewarm.

(continued)

2 Dissolve yeast in very warm water in large bowl. (Very warm water should feel comfortably warm when dropped on wrist.) Stir in cooled milk mixture and beaten egg.

3 Beat in 1 cup flour until smooth; beat in oil of anise. (Buy it at your drugstore.) Gradually beat in enough of remaining flour to make a stiff dough.

4 Turn out onto lightly floured pastry cloth or board; knead until smooth and elastic, adding only enough flour to keep dough from sticking.

5 Place dough in greased medium-size bowl; cover with clean towel; let rise in warm place, away from draft, 1 hour, or until double in bulk.

6 Tint uncooked eggs with Easter-egg coloring, following label directions; let dry while dough is rising.

7 Punch dough down; turn out onto lightly floured pastry cloth or board; divide into sixths. Roll each sixth into a rope, 12 inches long. Braid 3 ropes together on one side of a large cooky sheet; braid remaining ropes on other side. Form braids into one large circle, pinching ends together to make a tight seaL

8 Place each egg, large end up, in braid, spacing eggs evenly around ring. (The tiny air space in the large rounded end of the egg will keep it from cracking open during baking.) Cover with clean towel; let rise in warm place, away from draft, 1 hour or until double in bulk.

9 Bake in moderate oven (375°) 30 minutes, or until golden-brown; brush top with butter or margarine; serve warm.

Walnut Stickies

Bake them in rounds or squares

Bake at 375° for 40 minutes.
Makes 16 rolls.

DOUGH

    1 cup milk
    ¼ cup sugar
    ¾ teaspoon salt
    2 tablespoons vegetable shortening
    1 envelope active dry yeast
    ¼ cup very warm water
    1 egg, beaten
    2½ cups sifted all-purpose flour

TOPPING

    ¾ cup sugar
    ¾ cup water
    1 teaspoon ground cinnamon

    1 teaspoon grated orange rind
    ⅛ teaspoon salt
    1 cup chopped walnuts

FILLING

    4 tablespoons (½ stick) butter or margarine, melted
    ¼ cup sugar
    1 teaspoon ground cinnamon

1 Make dough: Scald milk with sugar, salt, and shortening in small saucepan; cool just until warm.

2 Sprinkle yeast into very warm water in large bowl. (Very warm water should feel comfortably warm when dropped on wrist.) Stir until yeast dissolves, then stir in cooled milk mixture. Beat in egg and 1½ cups of the flour until smooth; stir in remaining 1 cup flour to make a stiff dough.

3 Turn out onto lightly floured pastry cloth or board; knead until smooth and elastic, adding only enough flour to keep dough from sticking. Place in greased bowl; brush top lightly with shortening; cover with clean towel. Let rise in warm place, away from draft, 1 hour, or until double in bulk.

4 While dough rises, make topping: Combine sugar, water, cinnamon, orange rind, and salt in medium-size saucepan. Heat, stirring constantly, to boiling, then cook over medium heat 10 minutes, or until thick and syrupy. Pour half of the hot syrup into a greased baking pan, 8x8x2. (Or use a round 9-inch layer-cake pan.) Sprinkle evenly with walnuts. Set remaining syrup aside for glazing in Step 8.

5 To shape and fill rolls, punch dough down; turn out onto lightly floured pastry cloth or board. Roll out to a rectangle, 16x12. Spread generously with melted butter or margarine, then sprinkle with mixture of sugar and cinnamon.

6 Starting at long side of rectangle, roll up, jelly-roll style; cut crosswise into 16 slices. Place rolls, cut sides up, on nut-syrup mixture in pan.

7 Cover with clean towel; let rise in warm place, away from draft, 1 hour, or until double in bulk.

8 Bake in moderate oven (375°) 25 minutes. Remove from oven; spoon saved syrup over rolls. Bake 15 minutes longer, or until glazed and brown.

9 Cool in pan on wire rack 5 minutes; invert onto serving plate. Serve warm.

Almond Foldovers

These are pictured in the Convenience Bread Fix-Ups chapter

Bake at 350° for 20 minutes.
Makes 12 small loaves.

¾ cup milk
1 cup sugar
1 teaspoon salt
¾ cup (1½ sticks) butter or margarine
2 envelopes active dry yeast
¼ cup very warm water
2 eggs, beaten
5¼ cups sifted all-purpose flour
1½ cups golden raisins
1 container (8 ounces) candied red cherries, halved
1 teaspoon grated orange rind
1 can (8 ounces) almond paste
1 egg white, slightly beaten
10X (confectioners' powdered) sugar

1 Combine milk, ½ cup of the granulated sugar, salt, and ½ cup of the butter or margarine in a small saucepan. Heat slowly until butter or margarine melts; cool to lukewarm.
2 Sprinkle yeast into very warm water in a large bowl. (Very warm water should feel comfortably warm when dropped on wrist.) Stir until yeast dissolves, then stir in milk mixture and eggs.
3 Beat in 2 cups of the flour until smooth; stir in raisins, cherries, and orange rind. Beat in 3 cups more flour to make a stiff dough.
4 Turn out onto a lightly floured pastry cloth or board; knead until smooth and elastic, adding only enough of the remaining ¼ cup flour to keep dough from sticking.
5 Place in a greased large bowl; turn to coat all over with shortening; cover with a clean towel. Let rise in a warm place, away from draft, 2 hours, or until double in bulk.
6 While dough rises, crumble almond paste into a small bowl; stir in egg white and remaining ½ cup granulated sugar until smooth.
7 Punch dough down; knead a few times; divide into 12 even pieces. Pat each into an oval, 6x4, on a lightly floured pastry cloth or board; place, 2 inches apart, on greased large cooky sheets. Melt remaining ¼ cup butter or margarine in a small frying pan; brush part over ovals.
8 Divide almond mixture into 12 equal parts; with palms of hands, roll each into a 5-inch-long log. Place one lengthwise on half of each oval of dough; flatten slightly; fold dough in half. Press edges lightly to seal; cover. Let rise again, 1 hour, or until double in bulk. Brush with part of the remaining melted butter or margarine.

9 Bake in moderate oven (350°) 10 minutes; brush with remaining melted butter or margarine. Bake 10 minutes longer, or until golden, and loaves give a hollow sound when tapped. Remove from cooky sheets to wire racks; sprinkle with 10X sugar. Serve warm or cold.

Saint Lucia Saffron Buns

Sweden's famous Queen of Light festival inspired these dainty breakfast breads.

Bake at 400° for 12 minutes.
Makes 32 buns.

¼ cup milk
Pinch of saffron, crushed
¼ cup sugar
½ teaspoon salt
1 envelope active dry yeast
¼ cup very warm water
2 eggs
3 cups sifted all-purpose flour
½ cup (1 stick) butter or margarine, softened
Candied red and green cherries, cut in tiny squares
1 tablespoon cold water

1 Scald milk with saffron, sugar, and salt in a small saucepan; cool to lukewarm.
2 Sprinkle yeast into very warm water in a large bowl. (Very warm water should feel comfortably warm when dropped on wrist.) Stir until yeast dissolves, then stir in cooled milk mixture.
3 Beat eggs in a small bowl; save 1 tablespoonful for Step 5; beat remaining into yeast mixture. Stir in 1½ cups of the flour until smooth; beat in softened butter or margarine until completely blended, then beat in remaining flour to make a stiff dough. Knead until smooth and elastic on a lightly floured pastry cloth or board.
4 Place in a greased large bowl; cover with a clean towel. Let rise in a warm place, away from draft, 1 hour, or until double in bulk.
5 Punch dough down; knead several times; divide in quarters. Working with one at a time, roll into a rope; cut into 16 even-size pieces, then roll each into a 6-inch-long pencil-thin strip with hands. Cross each two strips on a greased large cooky sheet; curl each end into a small coil; decorate tip of each with a candied-cherry square. Repeat with remaining dough to make 32 buns. Cover; let rise again 30 minutes, or until double in bulk. Stir water into saved egg; brush over buns; sprinkle lightly with granulated sugar, if you wish.

(continued)

6 Bake in hot oven (400°) 12 minutes, or until golden-brown. Remove from cooky sheet; cool on wire racks. Serve warm or cold.

SAINT LUCIA SAFFRON BUNS

Plain arithmetic keeps these little sweets even in size. First divide long roll of dough into quarters, then each quarter in fourths again. Roll pieces into 6-inch-long "pencils"; cross each two "pencils" as shown, then curve ends into neat coil

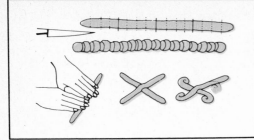

Crisscross Cinnamon Square and Frosted Cherry Cuplets

One batch of dough makes two different breakfast or coffeetime sweets

Bake at 375° for 25 minutes
for large coffeecake
and 15 minutes for tiny rolls.
Makes one 9-inch square coffeecake
and 4 dozen tiny rolls

½ cup milk
¾ cup sugar
1½ teaspoons salt
6 tablespoons (¾ stick) butter or margarine
2 envelopes active dry yeast
½ cup very warm water
2 eggs, slightly beaten
4½ cups sifted all-purpose flour
½ cup cherry jam (from a 12-ounce jar)
1 teaspoon ground cinnamon
½ cup sifted 10X (confectioners' powdered) sugar
1 tablespoon water

1 Scald milk with ½ cup of the sugar, salt and 4 tablespoons of the butter or margarine in a small saucepan; cool to lukewarm. (Set remaining ¼ cup sugar and 2 tablespoons butter or margarine aside for Step 12.)

2 Sprinkle yeast into very warm water in a large bowl. ("Very warm" water should feel comfortably warm when dropped on wrist.) Stir until yeast dissolves, then stir in cooled milk mixture and beaten eggs.

3 Beat in half of the flour until smooth, then beat in remaining to make a stiff dough.

4 Turn out onto a lightly floured pastry cloth or board; knead until smooth and elastic, adding only enough extra flour to keep dough from sticking.

5 Place in a greased large bowl; turn to coat all over with shortening; cover with a clean towel. Let rise in a warm place, away from draft, 1 hour, or until double in bulk.

6 Punch dough down; knead a few times; divide in half.

7 To shape CRISSCROSS CINNAMON SQUARE: Roll one half of dough to a rectangle, 9x8, on a lightly floured pastry cloth or board; cut into eight 1-inch-wide strips. Place 4 of the strips, about 1 inch apart, in a greased baking pan, 9x9x2. Weave in remaining 4 strips, over and under, to give a lattice effect; cover.

8 To shape FROSTED CHERRY CUPLETS: Roll out remaining half of dough to a 16-inch square; cut into rounds with a floured 2¼-inch cutter; reroll trimmings and cut out to make 48 rounds in all. Press rounds into greased tiny muffin-pan cups.

9 Spoon ½ teaspoonful cherry jam on top of each; cover.

10 Let both doughs rise again in a warm place, away from draft, 1 hour for large coffeecake and 30 minutes for rolls, or until each is double in bulk.

11 Bake small rolls in moderate oven (375°) 15 minutes, or until golden; remove from pans; cool on wire racks.

12 Melt remaining 2 tablespoons butter or margarine in a small frying pan; mix remaining ¼ cup sugar with cinnamon in a cup. Brush melted butter or margarine lightly over raised coffeecake dough; sprinkle with the cinnamon-sugar mixture.

13 Bake in moderate oven (375°) 25 minutes, or until richly browned and coffeecake gives a hollow sound when tapped. Loosen around edges with a knife; turn out onto a clean towel; turn right side up. Cool on a wire rack.

14 Combine 10X sugar with the 1 tablespoon water in a cup; drizzle over cherry rolls.

YEAST ROLLS

Fantans

Each roll separates easily—for buttering or coating with jelly

Bake at 375° for 20 minutes.
Makes 12 rolls.

¼ *recipe* FAVORITE YEAST ROLLS *(see index for recipe)*
2 *tablespoons butter or margarine, melted*

Roll out dough to an 18x9-inch rectangle on a lightly floured surface. Cut into twelve 1½-inch wide strips. Brush with melted butter. Stack 6 strips on top of each other to make two stacks. Cut each stack into six 1½-inch wide pieces. Place each piece of the cut stack, cut-side down, into a greased muffin-pan cup.

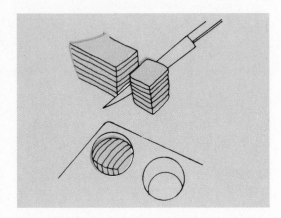

Crescent Rolls

Breakfast treats everybody will enjoy—there is no need of butter or jelly

Bake at 375° for 20 minutes.
Makes 16 or 24 rolls.

¼ *recipe* FAVORITE YEAST ROLLS *(see index for recipe)*
2 *tablespoons butter or margarine, melted*

Divide dough in half; roll out each half on a lightly floured surface to an 8-inch round; cut into 8 or 12 wedges. Brush wedges with melted butter. Roll up each wedge, starting at the large

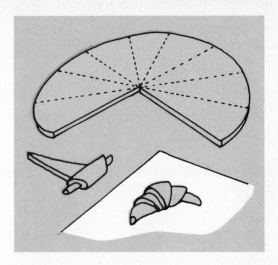

end; place, pointed-side down on an ungreased cookie sheet, curving the ends of the rolls slightly in order to shape as crescents.

Knots

They look difficult—but are easy to make

Bake at 375° for 20 minutes.
Makes 16 rolls.

¼ *recipe* FAVORITE YEAST ROLLS *(see index for recipe)*

Divide dough into 16 equal pieces. Roll each piece with palms of hands to a 6-inch rope on lightly floured surface. Tie a simple knot; form a loop, bring one end through. Place knots on greased cookie sheet 2 inches apart.

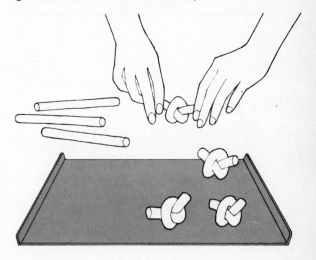

Cloverleaf Rolls

Pop your favorite jelly in the center

Bake at 375° for 20 minutes.
Makes 12 rolls.

¼ recipe FAVORITE YEAST ROLLS (see index for recipe)
2 tablespoons butter or margarine, melted

Divide dough into quarters and divide each quarter into 9 pieces to make 36 small pieces of dough. Shape dough into marble-size balls and place, 3 at a time, into greased muffin-pan cups; brush generously with butter.

OTHER SHAPES FOR YEAST ROLLS

Pan Rolls: Divide Favorite Yeast Roll into three equal parts and shape each into a fat sausage-like roll about 12 inches long. Slice each roll crosswise every 1 to 1½", roll slices into balls and place ¼" apart in greased 9-inch layer cake pans.

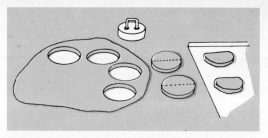

Parker House Rolls: Divide Favorite Yeast Roll into three equal parts and roll, one at a time, on a floured board into a circle 9 inches across. Cut into rounds with a lightly floured 2½-inch biscuit cutter; brush each round with softened butter or margarine, make a crease across each slightly to one side of center, then fold larger "half" over smaller, forming half moons, and place on greased baking sheets one inch apart. Pinch edges lightly to seal.

Quickie Cloverleaves: Pinch off pieces of Favorite Yeast Roll and roll into balls slightly larger than golf balls. Place in greased muffin-pan cups, then with kitchen shears, snip a cross into the top of each roll, forming "four-leaf clovers."

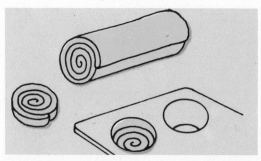

Pinwheels: Divide Favorite Yeast Roll into three equal parts and roll, one at a time, on a floured board into a rectangle 16 x 8 inches and about ¼ inch thick. Spread with softened butter or margarine and, if you like, cinnamon-sugar, jam or other filling. Roll up from the long side, jelly-roll style, then slice 1½ inches thick. Place pinwheels flat in greased muffin-pan cups.

Favorite Yeast Rolls

Golden, butter-melting rolls to serve hot from the oven—at breakfast, or any time! Bake a batch and freeze in serving-size portions

Bake at 375° for 20 minutes.
Makes about 5 dozen dinner-size rolls.

1½ cups milk
½ cup (1 stick) butter or margarine
¼ cup sugar
2 teaspoons salt
2 envelopes active dry yeast
1 teaspoon sugar
½ cup very warm water
2 eggs
8 cups sifted all-purpose flour

1 Heat milk with butter or margarine, ¼ cup sugar and salt in a small saucepan until butter melts; cool to lukewarm.
2 Sprinkle yeast into very warm water in a large bowl. (Very warm water should feel comfortably warm when dropped on wrist.) Stir in 1 teaspoon sugar. Stir until yeast dissolves. Let stand until bubbly and double in volume, about 10 minutes.
3 Stir in cooled milk mixture and beat in eggs. Beat in enough flour to make a soft dough; turn out onto lightly floured surface. Knead until smooth and elastic, about 5 minutes, adding only enough of the flour to keep the dough from sticking.
4 Place dough in a greased large bowl; turn to bring greased side up. Cover bowl with clean towel. Let rise in a warm place, away from drafts, 1½ hours, or until double in bulk.
5 Punch dough down; divide into quarters, keeping dough covered with an inverted bowl until ready to shape. Shape rolls in knots, crescents, etc. according to directions that follow. Place shaped rolls in greased baking pans. Cover rolls with a clean towel; let rise again in a warm place, away from drafts, 45 minutes, or until double in bulk.
6 Bake in moderate oven (375°) 20 minutes, or until golden. Brush tops lightly with butter, if you wish. Serve hot.

Sunday-Best Onion Rolls

Rapid mix method: Stir up dough the quick mixer way; then let it rise in the refrigerator until baking time

Bake at 375° for 30 minutes.
Makes 32 rolls.

6 to 7 cups sifted all-purpose flour
½ cup sugar
2 tablespoons instant minced onion
2 packages active dry yeast
1½ teaspoons salt
½ cup (1 stick) butter or margarine, softened
1½ cups very hot water
2 eggs
Vegetable oil

1 Measure 2 cups of the flour into a large bowl; stir in sugar, onion, yeast and salt. Add butter or margarine, then hot water, all at once.
2 Blend with electric mixer at low speed; then increase speed to medium and beat 2 minutes, scraping down side of bowl several times. Add eggs and 1 cup more flour; blend, then beat at high speed 1 minute, scraping down bowl once or twice.
3 Stir in just enough of the remaining flour to make a soft dough.
4 Turn out onto a lightly floured surface; knead 5 to 10 minutes, or until smooth and elastic, adding only enough flour to keep dough from sticking. Cover with plastic wrap, then a towel; let stand on surface 20 minutes.
5 Punch dough down; divide into quarters. Cut each quarter into 8 even pieces; shape each into a ball.
6 Measure 1 teaspoon vegetable oil into each of two 9x9x2-inch baking pans. Place 16 balls of dough in each pan, turning balls to coat with oil. Cover pans loosely with plastic wrap; chill from 2 to 24 hours.
7 When ready to bake, uncover; let stand at room temperature for 10 minutes.
8 Bake in moderate oven (375°) 30 minutes, or until rolls are golden. Remove from pans; cool a few minutes on a wire rack. If you prefer a softer crust, brush tops with butter or margarine. Serve warm.

EARLY-IN-THE-MORNING DANISH

Danish Pastry Dough I

The modern fast-to-make basic Danish dough

Makes 2 large pastries, or about 24 individual pastries,
or makes 1 large pastry and 12 individual pastries.

    2 envelopes active dry yeast
    ½ cup very warm water
    ⅓ cup sugar
    ¾ cup cold milk
    2 eggs
    4¼ cups sifted all-purpose flour
    1 teaspoon salt
    1 pound (4 sticks) butter or margarine
      Flour

1 Sprinkle yeast into very warm water in a 1-cup measure. (Very warm water should feel comfortably warm when dropped on wrist.) Stir in ½ teaspoon of the sugar. Stir until yeast dissolves. Let stand, undisturbed, until bubbly and double in volume, about 10 minutes.
2 Combine remaining sugar, milk, eggs, 3 cups of the flour, salt and the yeast mixture in large bowl. Beat with electric mixer at medium speed, for 3 minutes (or beat with spoon, 3 minutes). Beat in remaining flour with a wooden spoon until dough is shiny, elastic and soft. Scrape down sides of bowl. Cover with plastic wrap. Refrigerate 30 minutes.
3 Place the sticks of butter or margarine 1 inch apart, between 2 sheets of wax paper; roll out to a 12-inch square *(see Photo 1)*. Chill on a cookie sheet until ready to use.
4 Sprinkle working surface heavily with flour, about ⅓ cup; turn dough out onto flour *(see Photo 2)*; sprinkle flour on top of dough. Roll out to an 18x13-inch rectangle. Brush off excess flour with a soft pastry brush.
5 Peel off top sheet of wax paper from butter or margarine; place butter or margarine, paper side up on one end of dough to cover two-thirds of the dough; peel off remaining sheet of wax paper. For easy folding, carefully score butter lengthwise down center, without cutting into dough. Fold uncovered third of dough over middle third *(see Photo 3)*; brush off excess flour; then fold remaining third of dough over middle third to enclose butter completely. Turn dough clockwise so open side is away from you.
6 *Roll out to a 24x12-inch rectangle using enough flour to keep dough from sticking. Fold ends in to meet on center *(see Photo 4)*; then fold dough in half to make 4 layers. Turn again so open side is away from you *(see Photo 5)*.
*Repeat rolling and folding this way 2 more times. Keep the dough to a perfect rectangle by rolling straight up and down and from side to side. When it is necessary, chill the dough between rollings. [**Note:** If using margarine, which is of a softer consistency than butter, refrigerate 20 minutes between each rolling.] Clean off the working surface each time and dust lightly with flour. Refrigerate dough 1 hour or more (even overnight, if you wish, to relax dough and firm up butter layers). Cut dough in half *(see Photo 6)*, you can see the buttery layers, which when baked, become flaky and crisp. Work with only half the dough at a time. Keep the other half refrigerated until ready to use *(see Photo 7)*.

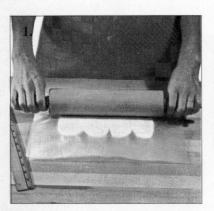

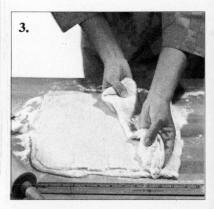

Fruit-Filled Danish (Svedske Konvolut)

Light, flaky Danish bursting with fruit. Use prune filling, as indicated, or try canned cherry or apple pie filling, or apricot preserves for interesting variations

Preheat oven to 400°; bake at 350°, 25 minutes.
Makes 12 individual pastries.

½ DANISH PASTRY DOUGH I *(see index for recipe)*
 1 *can (12 ounces) prune filling*
  OR: 1 jar (8 ounces) Lekvar
  OR: 1 can (about 1 pound, 5 ounces) other fruit filling
  OR: Apricot preserves
  Slightly beaten egg
½ *cup corn syrup*

1 Roll dough and cut into squares as in ALMOND CRESCENTS (see index). Spoon a rounded tablespoon of prune or other fruit filling onto center of each square; bring 2 opposite corners over filling to overlap about 1 inch.
2 Place on a cookie sheet 2 inches apart; let rise in a warm place in your kitchen, until double in bulk, about 30 minutes. (*Not* in your oven, or over hot water, as with other yeast breads; the extra heat will melt the butter and ruin the texture of the Danish pastry.) Brush with beaten egg.
3 Place in a hot oven (400°); lower heat to 350° immediately, then bake 20 minutes. Warm corn syrup slightly in a small saucepan; brush over pastries; bake 5 minutes longer. Remove to wire rack; cool.

Almond Crescents (Mandelhorn)

Easy to shape; delicious to eat—almond flavor inside and out

Pre-heat oven to 400°; bake at 350°
for 20 minutes.
Makes 12 individual pastries.

½ DANISH PASTRY DOUGH I *(see index for recipe)*
 ALMOND FILLING *(see index for recipe)*
 Slightly beaten egg
 Sugar
 Sliced Almonds

(continued)

1 Roll pastry on floured surface to a 20x15-inch rectangle; trim edges evenly. With a sharp knife, cut into twelve 5-inch squares. Spoon an equal amount of filling onto one corner of each square. Roll pastry dough around filling; continue rolling to opposite corner. Place pastries point down, 2 inches apart on cookie sheet. Curve into crescent shapes.

2 Let rise in a warm place in your kitchen, until double in bulk, about 30 minutes. (*Not* in your oven, or over hot water, as with other yeast breads; the extra heat will melt the butter and ruin the texture of the Danish pastry.) Brush with egg; sprinkle with sugar and almonds.

3 Place in a hot oven (400°); lower heat immediately to 350°; then bake 20 minutes, or until puffed and golden. Remove to wire rack; cool.

Cockscombs (Hanekam)

Distinctively shaped pastries with an almond filling

Preheat oven to 400°; bake at 350° for 20 minutes. Makes 12 individual pastries.

½ DANISH PASTRY DOUGH I *(see index for recipe)*
ALMOND FILLING *(see index for recipe)*
Slightly beaten egg
Sugar

1 Roll and cut dough as in ALMOND CRESCENTS. Spoon an equal amount of filling onto the center of each square. Spread filling parallel to one edge; brush edges lightly with egg, then fold opposite edge over; press edges together to seal. Make 4 or 5 slits in sealed edge; place on cookie sheets, curving pastries slightly to resemble a cockscomb.

2 Let rise in a warm place in your kitchen, until double in bulk, about 30 minutes. (*Not* in your oven, or over hot water, as with other yeast breads; the extra heat will melt the butter and ruin the texture of the Danish pastry.) Brush with egg; sprinkle generously with sugar.

3 Place in a hot oven (400°); lower heat immediately to 350°. Bake 20 minutes, or until puffed and golden brown. Remove pastries to wire rack; cool completely.

Apricot Bow Ties (Abrikos Sløjfe)

A walnut topping and sweet apricot filling combine for a delectable taste treat

Preheat oven to 400°; bake at 350°, 20 minutes. Makes 12 individual pastries.

½ DANISH PASTRY DOUGH I *(see index for recipe)*
Apricot preserves
Slightly beaten egg
2 tablespoons chopped walnuts mixed with 2 tablespoons sugar

1 Roll and cut dough as in ALMOND CRESCENTS. Place 1 teaspoon of the apricot preserves along one of the edges of the pastry ½ inch in from edge. Fold over opposite edge; press edges together to seal. With a sharp knife, make a lengthwise slit in folded pastry to within 1 inch of each end. Slip one end under and pull it through the slit. Place pastries 2 inches apart on cookie sheets.

2 Let rise in a warm place in your kitchen, until double in bulk, 30 to 45 minutes. (*Not* in your oven, or over hot water, as in other yeast breads; the extra heat will melt the butter and ruin the texture of the Danish pastry.) Brush with egg; sprinkle with walnut mixture.

3 Place in a hot oven (400°); lower heat immediately to 350°. Bake 20 minutes or until golden. Cool on wire racks.

Mayor's Braid (Borgmestor Krans)

Large, almond-and-sugar sprinkled—a Danish delight

Preheat oven to 400°, then bake at 350° for 40 minutes. Makes one 10-inch round pastry.

½ DANISH PASTRY DOUGH I *(see index for recipe)*
ALMOND FILLING *(see index for recipe)*
Slightly beaten egg
Sugar
Sliced almonds

1 Roll dough on a floured surface to a 30x9-inch rectangle; cut lengthwise into 3 strips. Spread equal amounts of filling down the center of each strip. Fold edges of strips over filling to enclose filling completely. Press ends of the 3 filled strips together; braid; press other ends together. Ease braid onto an ungreased cookie sheet; join ends together to make a ring, about 9 inches in diameter.

2 Let rise in a warm place in your kitchen, about 45 minutes, or until double in bulk. (*Not* in your oven, or over a bowl of hot water, as with other yeast breads; the extra heat will melt the butter and ruin the texture of the Danish pastry.) Brush with egg; sprinkle generously with sugar and almonds.

3 Place in a hot oven (400°); lower heat immediately to 350°. Bake 40 minutes or until puffed and golden; remove to a wire rack; cool. Cut into wedges to serve. This pastry is rich and will spread when baked. You may wish to place a collar of foil around the pastry just before baking to keep it more compact.

DANISH HOW-TO

Here are some helpful how-to's for making and baking delicious Danish:

• *Before you begin to make Danish, be sure you have a working surface large enough to roll dough to 30 inches.*

• *Use more flour on your rolling surface than you would when rolling out other types of dough. Be sure you brush off excess flour with a soft pastry brush immediately before folding and filling, so excess flour won't build up in pastry.*

• *It is important to keep butter or margarine enclosed in dough, while rolling Danish. If butter or margarine oozes out, immediately sprinkle with flour. Also, if dough becomes too sticky to handle, it's probably because butter has softened. In both cases, chill for 30 minutes before continuing rolling and folding.*

• *For freezing unbaked Danish: Place shaped Danish on cookie sheets. Don't brush with egg or sprinkle with toppings. Cover with plastic wrap; freeze.*

• *To bake: Remove Danish from freezer the night before you plan to bake it, and place in refrigerator. Next morning, arrange on cookie sheets, 2 inches apart. Let rise, according to recipe instructions, until double in volume. Then brush with egg; sprinkle with topping; bake following individual recipes.*

• *For refrigerating unbaked Danish: Place shaped Danish on cookie sheets; cover; refrigerate.*

• *To bake: Next day, remove Danish from refrigerator; let rise and bake, as above.*

Breakfast in bed is an exquisite treat, especially when you can munch on **Elephant Ears** and imagine yourself on a safari.

Elephant Ears (Elefantører)

Try these classic pastries swirled with Sugar Icing

Preheat oven to 400°; bake at 350°, 20 minutes.
Makes 12 individual pastries.

½ DANISH PASTRY DOUGH I *(see index for recipe)*
CINNAMON-PECAN FILLING *(recipe follows)*
Slightly beaten egg
Sugar
Coarsely chopped pecans

1 Roll pastry to a 12x12-inch square; spread filling evenly over pastry; roll up jelly roll fashion. With a sharp knife, cut into 1-inch pieces, then carefully cut each piece in half, but not all the way through. Spread out the 2 halves, leaving them attached in the center; place 2 inches apart on cookie sheets.

2 Let rise in a warm place in your kitchen until double in bulk, about 30 to 45 minutes. (*Not* in your oven or over hot water, as with other yeast breads; the extra heat will melt the butter and ruin texture of the Danish pastry.) Brush with egg; sprinkle with sugar and pecans.

3 Place in a hot oven (400°); lower heat immediately to 350°. Bake 20 to 25 minutes, or until puffed and golden brown. Remove to wire rack; cool.

(continued)

It doesn't have to be a fancy brunch for you to fix **Cheese Danish.** Just any time will do to delight your spouse with this quick-to-fix sprightly breakfast.

SUGAR ICING

Combine ½ cup 10X (confectioners') sugar with 1 tablespoon warm water. Drizzle over baked Danish with the top of a teaspoon.

CINNAMON-PECAN FILLING

Makes 1 cup.

Beat 4 tablespoons softened butter or margarine, ½ cup sugar, ½ teaspoon ground cinnamon and ½ teaspoon ground cardamom in a small bowl until smooth. Stir in ½ cup coarsely chopped pecans and ¼ cup currants.

Cheese Danish (Spandauer)

Bright cherry glaze adds a colorful finishing touch to these coffee-time favorites

Preheat oven to 400°; bake at 350°, 20 minutes. Makes 12 individual pastries.

½ DANISH PASTRY DOUGH I *(see index for recipe)*
 CREAM CHEESE FILLING *(see index)*
 Cherry preserves
 Slightly beaten egg
½ *cup corn syrup*

1 Roll and cut dough as in ALMOND CRESCENTS. Spoon equal amounts of CHEESE FILLING onto the center of each square; fold in all 4 corners to meet and overlap slightly in center, to enclose filling completely; press points down with fingertip.
2 Place 2 inches apart on cookie sheet; let rise in a warm place in your kitchen, until double in bulk, about 30 minutes. (*Not* in your oven, or over hot water, as with other yeast breads; the extra heat will melt the butter and ruin the texture of the Danish pastry.) Press down points again and fill center with a teaspoon of cherry preserves. Brush pastry with egg.
3 Place in a hot oven (400°); lower heat immediately to 350°. Bake 20 minutes, or until puffed and golden brown. Heat corn syrup just until warm; brush over pastries. Remove to wire rack; cool. Add more preserves after pastries are baked, if you wish. Pastries will open up as they bake.

Basic Danish Pastry Dough II

Longer to make than Danish Pastry Dough I, but a more classic version

 3 envelopes active dry yeast
½ *cup very warm water*
¾ *cup milk*
 1 egg
⅓ *cup sugar*
 1 teaspoon salt
 4 cups sifted all-purpose flour
¾ *pound (3 sticks) very cold butter or margarine*

1 Sprinkle yeast into very warm water in a large bowl. (Very warm water should feel comfortably warm when dropped on wrist.) Stir until yeast dissolves, then stir in milk, egg, sugar, and salt.
2 Stir in 3¼ cups of the flour to make a soft dough. (Set remaining ¾ cup flour aside for next

step.) Beat dough vigorously about 2 minutes, or 300 strokes or until shiny and elastic.

3 Sprinkle pastry cloth or board with ⅔ of the remaining flour. Turn out dough; form into a flat ball; sprinkle with remaining flour. Roll out to a rectangle, 18x12.

4 Slice the *very cold* butter or margarine into thin strips lengthwise; place over ⅔ of the dough to form a 12-inch square.

5 Fold dough, brushing off excess flour each time, this way: Fold unbuttered third over middle third, then opposite end over top. Now fold into thirds crosswise to make a block, 6x4. It will be 9 layers deep. Repeat rolling and folding as above 3 times more. (This gives the pastry its buttery-rich flakiness when baked.) Unless the dough gets too soft to handle easily, there is no need to chill it between the 3 rollings.

6 Now dough is ready to shape, fill, and bake, according to your choice of recipes.

Pinwheels

In Denmark, this classic has many fillings. Our choice is almond with strawberry jam

Preheat oven to 450°, then lower
heat to 375° and bake for 15 minutes.
Makes 2 dozen

BASIC DANISH PASTRY DOUGH II
ALMOND FILLING *(recipe follows)*
1 teaspoon strawberry jam
1 egg
Sugar

1 Roll out BASIC DANISH PASTRY DOUGH II to a rectangle, 16x24, on a lightly floured pastry cloth or board. Cut lengthwise into quarters, then crosswise into sixths to make 24 four-inch squares. Starting at each corner, cut through pastry 1½ inches in toward center.

2 Place 1 teaspoonful ALMOND FILLING in center of each square, then top with 1 teaspoonful strawberry jam. Pick up every other corner point and fold to center, overlapping points slightly and pinching together to hold, to make a pin-wheel.

3 Place, 4 inches apart, on greased cookie sheets. Cover; let rise in a warm place, away from drafts, 1 hour, or until double in bulk. Brush tops with slightly beaten egg; sprinkle lightly with sugar.

4 Place in very hot oven (450°); lower heat to moderate (375°) at once. Bake 15 minutes, or until golden-brown.

ALMOND FILLING

Makes about ⅔ cup.

Beat 1 egg white slightly in a small bowl. Stir in ½ cup almond paste (from an 8-ounce can) and ½ cup sugar. Mix lightly with a fork until well-blended.

Sugared Fans

BASIC DANISH PASTRY DOUGH II
Jam
OR: CREAM CHEESE FILLING *(recipe follows)*
1 egg
Sugar

1 Roll out BASIC DANISH PASTRY DOUGH II to a rectangle, 16x24, on a lightly floured pastry cloth or board. Cut lengthwise into quarters, then crosswise into sixths to make 24 four-inch squares.

2 Place a generous tablespoonful of your choice of jam or CREAM-CHEESE FILLING across middle of each square; fold dough over and press edges together to seal. Cut about 4 slits, each ¾ inch long, in sealed edge; curve folded edge into a fan shape.

3 Place, 4 inches apart, on greased cookie sheets. Cover; let rise in a warm place, away from draft, 1 hour, or until double in bulk. Brush tops with slightly beaten egg; sprinkle generously with sugar.

4 Place in very hot oven (450°); lower heat to moderate (375°) at once. Bake 15 minutes, or until golden-brown.

Cheese Squares

Each square, folded envelope style, hides a cream-cheese filling

Preheat oven to 450°, then lower
heat to 375° and bake for 15 minutes.
Makes 2 dozen

BASIC DANISH PASTRY DOUGH II
CREAM CHEESE FILLING *(recipe follows)*
1 egg
Sugar

1 Roll out BASIC DANISH PASTRY DOUGH II to a rectangle, 16x24, on a lightly floured pastry cloth or board. Cut lengthwise into quarters,

(continued)

When it's partytime, think of Danish. Use one basic recipe—different fillings and your own bread sculpture are all that is necessary for this tantalizing array of Danish pastries.

then crosswise into sixths to make 24 four-inch squares.

2 Place 1 tablespoonful CREAM-CHEESE FILLING in middle of each. Fold all 4 corners, overlapping slightly, to center to cover filling completely; press together to seal. (Edges will open during baking.)

3 Place, 3 inches apart, on greased cookie sheets. Cover; let rise in a warm place, away from drafts, 1 hour, or until double in bulk. Brush tops with slightly beaten egg; sprinkle lightly with sugar.

4 Place in very hot oven (450°); lower heat to moderate (375°) at once. Bake 15 minutes, or until golden-brown.

CREAM-CHEESE FILLING

Makes about 2 cups.

Combine 2 packages (8 ounces each) cream cheese, ¼ cup sugar, and 2 tablespoons lemon juice in a medium-size bowl; beat until blended.

Danish Twists

BASIC DANISH PASTRY DOUGH II
½ *cup* ALMOND FILLING *(see index for recipe)*
1 *egg*
Sugar

Preheat oven to 450°, then lower heat to 375° and bake for 12 to 15 minutes. Makes 3 dozen.

1 Divide BASIC DANISH PASTRY DOUGH II in half; chill or freeze one half to make into more twists or *Cream Buns,* if you wish. Roll out the remaining half to a rectangle, 18x10, on a lightly floured pastry cloth or board; cut in half crosswise.

2 Spread one half with about ½ cup ALMOND FILLING; top with second half, then cut in half crosswise to make two rectangles, each 9x5. Cut each crosswise into 18 one-half-inch-wide strips. Lift strips, 1 at a time, and twist carefully

3 or 4 times. Place, 3 inches apart, on greased cookie sheets.

3 Cover; let rise in a warm place, away from draft, 1 hour, or until double in bulk. Brush tops with slightly beaten egg; sprinkle lightly with sugar.

4 Place in very hot oven (450°); lower heat to moderate (375°) at once. Bake 12 to 15 minutes, or until golden-brown.

Jam Foldovers

BASIC DANISH PASTRY DOUGH II
½ cup VANILLA-CREAM FILLING *(recipe follows)*
¼ cup raspberry jam
¼ cup pineapple jam
1 egg
Sugar

1 Roll out BASIC DANISH PASTRY DOUGH II to a rectangle, 16x24, on a lightly floured pastry cloth or board. Cut lengthwise into quarters, then crosswise into sixths to make 24 four-inch squares.

2 Place 1 teaspoonful VANILLA-CREAM FILLING in center of each and ½ teaspoonful each of raspberry and pineapple jams on either side. Fold one corner over filling to cover, then fold opposite corner over top. (Jams will show at either end and edges will open during baking.) Place, 4 inches apart, on greased cookie sheets.

3 Cover; let rise in a warm place, away from drafts, 1 hour, or until double in bulk. Brush tops with slightly beaten egg; sprinkle lightly with sugar.

4 Place in very hot oven (450°); lower heat to moderate (375°) at once. Bake 15 minutes, or until golden-brown.

VANILLA-CREAM FILLING

Mix 2 tablespoons sugar and 2 tablespoons cornstarch in top of a small double boiler; stir in 1 egg yolk, then beat in 1 cup milk. Cook, stirring constantly, over simmering water 10 minutes, or until mixture thickens, then continue cooking, without stirring, 5 minutes longer. Pour into a small bowl; stir in 1 teaspoon vanilla; cool. Makes 1 cup.

Whirligig Custard Cake

Rich cream-and-raisin filling goes between the base and pinwheel top of this beauty

Preheat oven to 450°, then lower heat to 350° and bake for 40 minutes. Makes 1 eight-inch round cake

BASIC DANISH PASTRY DOUGH II
⅓ cup VANILLA-CREAM FILLING *(see index for recipe)*
¼ cup seedless raisins
BUTTER CREAM FILLING *(recipe follows)*
1 egg
10X (confectioners' powdered) sugar

1 Divide BASIC DANISH PASTRY DOUGH II into thirds; chill or freeze two thirds to make into more cakes or FRUIT-CREAM TRIANGLES, if you wish. Roll out remaining third to a rectangle, 16x8, on a lightly floured pastry cloth or board; divide in half crosswise to make 2 eight-inch squares. Fit one square into the bottom of a greased 8-inch spring-form pan. (No need to cut dough into a circle as it is soft enough to shape easily.)

2 Spread with ⅓ cup VANILLA-CREAM FILLING; sprinkle with ¼ cup seedless raisins. Spread remaining 8-inch square with BUTTER-CREAM FILLING. Roll up, jelly-roll fashion, then slice crosswise into 7 even-size rounds.

3 Place, cut side up, on top of filling. Cover; let rise in a warm place, away from drafts, 1 hour, or until double in bulk. Brush top with slightly beaten egg.

4 Place in very hot oven (450°); lower heat to moderate (350°) at once. Bake 40 minutes, or until golden-brown. Cool 5 minutes on a wire rack; release spring and lift off side of pan, leaving cake on its metal base. Serve plain or sprinkle with 10X (confectioners' powdered) sugar.

BUTTER-CREAM FILLING

Makes ¼ cup.

Cream 4 tablespoons (½ stick) butter or margarine with ¼ cup sugar until fluffy in a small bowl; stir in ½ teaspoon almond extract.

Memorable Moments With Quick Breads

Pour batters, drop batters, and soft doughs. These are all quick bread mixtures. Pour batters are used for light-as-a-feather pancakes and robust waffles; drop batters form the basis for dumplings, fruit and nut loaves, and many coffee cakes; and biscuits, scones, and doughnuts start off as soft dough. Whichever you want to make, you'll find many examples in this chapter.

BREADS

Lemon Tea Loaf

Sparkly lemon sugar glazes the top of this mellow bread as it cools. Candied fruit slices are a pretty holiday trim

Bake at 350° for 1 hour and 15 minutes.
Makes 1 loaf, 9x5x3

    3 cups sifted all-purpose flour
    ¾ cup granulated sugar (for bread)
    3 teaspoons baking powder
    1 teaspoon salt
    ¼ teaspoon baking soda
    ¼ teaspoon ground nutmeg
    ½ cup finely chopped walnuts
    ¼ cup firmly packed brown sugar
    1 tablespoon grated lemon rind
    1 egg
  1¼ cups milk
    4 tablespoons (½ stick) butter or margarine, melted
    1 tablespoon granulated sugar (for topping)
    1 tablespoon lemon juice

1 Sift flour, the ¼ cup granulated sugar, baking powder, salt, soda and nutmeg into a large bowl; stir in walnuts, brown sugar and lemon rind.

Muffins make the meal, morning, noon, and night. Here are three choice ones you'll enjoy anytime of day: **Blueberry Muffins, Corn Muffins,** and **Whole Wheat Muffins.**

2 Beat egg slightly with milk in a small bowl; stir in melted butter or margarine; pour all at once into flour mixture. Stir about 30 strokes, or just until evenly moist. Spoon into a well-greased loaf pan, 9x5x3; let stand 20 minutes.
3 Bake in moderate oven (350°) 1 hour and 15 minutes, or until a wooden pick inserted in center comes out clean.
4 Cool in pan on a wire rack 5 minutes; turn out onto rack.
5 Mix the 1 tablespoon granulated sugar and lemon juice in a cup; brush over top of loaf several times to glaze. Cool loaf completely; wrap and store at least a day before slicing.
6 Just before serving or giving, trim with CANDIED LEMON SLICES (directions follow), if you wish.

CANDIED LEMON SLICES
Sprinkle 2 tablespoons granulated sugar on a flat plate; place 4 slices lemon in a single layer on top; sprinkle with 2 more tablespoons sugar. Let stand at room temperature, turning two or three times, 2 hours, or until richly glazed. Remove and let dry on wax paper. Decorate center of each with a candied-cherry half.

Banana-Nut Bread

The luscious bananas and crunchy nuts in this classic loaf make a moist bread with great texture

Bake at 325° for 1 hour and 20 minutes.
Makes one 9x5x3-inch loaf.

  2⅔ cups sifted all-purpose flour
    3 teaspoons baking powder
    1 teaspoon salt
    ¼ teaspoon baking soda
    ½ cup (1 stick) butter or margarine
    1 cup sugar
    3 eggs
    2 medium-size ripe bananas, peeled and mashed (about 1 cup)
    ¾ cup pecans, finely chopped
    2 teaspoons grated orange rind

(continued)

A bread for all seasons, **Banana-Nut Bread** is both rich and moist.

1 Grease a 9x5x3-inch loaf pan, line bottom with wax paper; grease paper.
2 Sift flour, baking powder, salt and baking soda onto a sheet of wax paper.
3 In a large bowl, cream butter or margarine with sugar, until fluffy. Beat in eggs, one at a time, until fluffy again.
4 Stir in flour mixture, alternately with mashed bananas; fold in pecans and orange rind. Pour into prepared pan.
5 Bake in a slow oven (325°) 1 hour and 20 minutes, or until golden, and a wooden pick inserted in the center comes out clean. Cool in pan on a wire rack 10 minutes. Loosen around edges with a knife; turn out onto rack; peel off waxed paper. Let cool completely. Wrap and store overnight.

Date Tea Bread

It's dark, moist, and mellow-rich

Bake at 350° for 1 hour and 10 minutes.
Makes 1 loaf, 9x5x3

  1 *package (8 ounces) pitted dates*
1¼ *cups boiling water*
1½ *cups firmly packed brown sugar*
  6 *tablespoons (¾ stick) butter or margarine*
  1 *egg, beaten*

2¼ *cups sifted all-purpose flour*
1½ *teaspoons baking soda*
1½ *teaspoons salt*

1 Cut dates in small pieces into medium-size bowl; pour boiling water over. Stir in sugar and butter or margarine until butter melts; cool. Stir in beaten egg.
2 Sift flour, soda, and salt onto wax paper; stir into date mixture just until blended. Pour into greased loaf pan, 9x5x3; let stand 15 minutes.
3 Bake in moderate oven (350°) 1 hour and 10 minutes, or until wooden pick inserted deep into loaf comes out clean. Cool in pan 5 minutes; turn out on wire rack; cool completely.
4 Wrap in wax paper, foil, or transparent wrap; store at least 1 day before slicing.

Pineapple-Cherry Bread

Accompany with a gelatin salad or a mound of chilled custard

Bake at 350° for 1 hour and 15 minutes.
Makes 1 loaf, 9x5x3.

3 *cups sifted all-purpose flour*
4 *teaspoons baking powder*
¾ *cup sugar*
1 *teaspoon salt*

1 cup chopped walnuts
½ cup candied cherries, halved
1 egg
1 can (about 8 ounces) crushed pineapple
½ cup milk
¼ cup vegetable oil

1 Grease a loaf pan, 9x5x3.
2 Sift flour, baking powder, sugar and salt into a large bowl; stir in walnuts and cherries.
3 Beat egg well in a medium-size bowl; stir in pineapple and syrup, milk and vegetable oil. Add all at once to flour mixture; stir just until evenly moist. Spoon into prepared pan; spread top even.
4 Bake in moderate oven (350°) 1 hour and 15 minutes, or until a wooden pick inserted in center comes out clean. Cool in pan on a wire rack 10 minutes. Loosen around edges with a knife; turn out onto rack. Cool completely.
5 Wrap loaf in wax paper, foil or transparent wrap. Store overnight to mellow flavors.

Mince Loaf

An old-fashioned favorite that is still popular

Bake at 350° for 1 hour.
Makes 1 loaf, 9x5x3.

3 cups sifted all-purpose flour
3½ teaspoons baking powder
½ teaspoon salt
¼ teaspoon baking soda
¾ cup firmly packed brown sugar
1½ cups chopped walnuts
2 eggs
½ cup milk
⅓ cup vegetable oil
1 cup prepared mincemeat (from a 1-pound, 12-ounce jar)

1 Grease a loaf pan, 9x5x3.
2 Sift flour, baking powder, salt and soda into a large bowl; stir in brown sugar and walnuts.
3 Beat eggs well in a small bowl; stir in milk, vegetable oil and mincemeat. Add all at once to flour mixture; stir just until evenly moist. Spoon into prepared pan; spread top even.
4 Bake in moderate oven (350°) 1 hour, or until a wooden pick inserted in center comes out clean. Cool in pan on a wire rack 10 minutes. Loosen around edges with a knife; turn out onto rack. Cool completely.
5 Wrap loaf in wax paper, foil or transparent wrap. Store overnight to mellow flavors.

Honey-Spice Ring

Light as spongecake, this loaf is flecked with candied orange peel

Bake at 350° for 45 minutes.
Makes 1 nine-inch ring

2 cups sifted all-purpose flour
1 teaspoon ground cloves
1 teaspoon ground ginger
½ teaspoon baking powder
4 eggs
1 cup firmly packed brown sugar
⅓ cup honey
¼ cup coarsely chopped candied orange peel

1 Sift flour, spices, and baking powder onto wax paper.
2 Beat eggs until foamy in a large bowl; sprinkle in brown sugar, beating until fluffy; beat in honey. (Beating will take about 15 minutes altogether with an electric beater.)
3 Fold in orange peel, then flour mixture just until blended. Spoon into an ungreased 9-inch tube pan.
4 Bake in moderate oven (350°) 45 minutes, or until top springs back when pressed with fingertip. Invert pan, hanging tube over a bottle; cool bread completely.
5 Remove from pan to a serving plate. Cut in thin wedges.

Apple-Walnut Bread

There's a hint of cinnamon, for extra flavor

Bake at 350° for 1 hour and 10 minutes.
Makes 1 loaf, 9x5x3.

3 cups sifted all-purpose flour
¾ cup sugar
3 teaspoons baking powder
1 teaspoon salt
½ teaspoon ground cinnamon
2 cups diced, pared and cored apple
½ cup finely chopped walnuts
1 egg
¾ cup milk
3 tablespoons vegetable shortening, melted

1 Sift flour, sugar, baking powder, salt, and cinnamon into a large bowl; stir in diced apple and walnuts to mix well. Beat the egg slightly with milk and shortening in a small bowl

(continued)

2 Pour all at once into flour mixture; stir just until evenly moist. (Work with a light hand, for heavy—or too much—stirring will cause the baked bread to have small tunnels in it)

3 Spoon batter into a well-greased loaf pan, 9x5x3, then spread to sides of pan with a spoon, leaving a slight well in center. This helps loaf rise evenly with no hump in middle

4 Bake in moderate oven (350°) 1 hour and 10 minutes, or until wooden pick inserted in center comes out clean and loaf pulls away from sides of pan. Remove from pan; cool

Cinnamon-Prune Bread

The combination is unusual—but you'll not regret baking this fruit bread

Bake at 350° for 1 hour and 5 minutes.
Makes 1 loaf, 9x5x3.

  1 cup pitted prunes, chopped (from a 12-ounce package)
  ½ cup boiling water
  3 cups sifted all-purpose flour
4½ teaspoons baking powder
  ½ teaspoon salt
  ½ teaspoon ground cinnamon
  ⅔ cup firmly packed brown sugar
  1 tablespoon grated orange rind
  1 cup chopped pecans
  1 egg
  ¼ cup vegetable oil
  ¾ cup milk

1 Grease a loaf pan, 9x5x3.

2 Combine prunes and boiling water in a small bowl; let stand while preparing batter.

3 Sift flour, baking powder, salt, and cinnamon into a large bowl; stir in brown sugar, orange rind, and pecans.

4 Beat egg well in a medium-size bowl; stir in vegetable oil, milk, and prune mixture. Add all at once to flour mixture; stir just until evenly moist. Spoon into prepared pan; spread top even.

5 Bake in moderate oven (350°) 1 hour and 5 minutes, or until a wooden pick inserted in center comes out clean. Cool in pan on a wire rack 10 minutes. Loosen around edges with a knife; turn out onto rack. Cool completely.

6 Wrap loaf in wax paper, foil, or transparent wrap. Store overnight to mellow flavors and make slicing easier. Cut in thin slices.

Cranberry-Pecan Bread

No need to ice this cranberry-filled bread—chopped pecans make the interesting crust

Bake at 350° for 1 hour and 10 minutes.
Makes 1 nine-inch round loaf.

1½ cups chopped pecans
1½ cups coarsely ground cranberries
1¼ cups sugar
  3 cups sifted all-purpose flour
4½ teaspoons baking powder
  ½ teaspoon salt
  ½ cup vegetable shortening
  2 teaspoons grated lemon rind
  2 eggs
  1 cup milk

1 Grease a 9-inch angel-cake pan; sprinkle ½ cup of the pecans over the bottom.

2 Mix cranberries and ¼ cup of the sugar in a small bowl; let stand while preparing batter.

3 Sift flour, remaining 1 cup sugar, baking powder, and salt into a large bowl; cut in shortening with a pastry blender until mixture resembles corn meal. Stir in remaining 1 cup pecans and lemon rind.

4 Beat eggs well in a small bowl; stir in milk. Add all at once to flour mixture; stir just until evenly moist. Spoon into prepared pan; spread top even.

5 Bake in moderate oven (350°) 1 hour and 10 minutes, or until a wooden pick inserted near center comes out clean. Cool in pan on a wire rack 10 minutes. Loosen around edge and center with a knife; turn out onto rack. Cool loaf completely.

6 Wrap loaf in wax paper, foil, or transparent wrap. Store overnight to mellow flavors and make slicing easier. Cut in thin wedges.

Whether on the buffet, in the middle of the dining table, or temptingly on the kitchen counter, **Cranberry-Pecan Bread** is a star.

Old-Fashioned Corn Bread

Leave to the last minute—from measuring cup to the table in only 25 minutes

> Bake at 425° for 20 minutes.
> Makes 12 sticks, 12 muffins,
> or 1 nine-inch square loaf.

1½ cups yellow or white corn meal
1½ teaspoons baking powder
 1 teaspoon salt
 ¾ teaspoon baking soda
 1 egg
1½ cups buttermilk
 ¼ cup vegetable shortening, melted

1 Measure dry ingredients into large bowl; mix with a fork. (No need to sift corn meal.) Beat egg into buttermilk; stir in to make a thin smooth batter
2 Pour melted shortening into cornmeal mixture; stir to blend. To make crust crisp, heat greased corn-stick, muffin, or 9x9x2 pan while mixing up batter
3 Pour batter in hot pan. Bake in hot oven (425°) 20 minutes for sticks and muffins, 25 minutes for square loaf, or until crusty and golden-brown. Serve hot

Country Corn Bread

Warm and golden, this Southern favorite is absolutely delicious spread with soft butter and homemade jelly

> Bake at 450° for 25 minutes.
> Makes two 8x8x2-inch breads.

1½ cups yellow cornmeal
 2 cups sifted all-purpose flour
 2 tablespoons sugar
 4 teaspoons baking powder
 1 teaspoon salt
 2 eggs
 2 cups milk
 4 tablespoons bacon drippings or shortening

1 Combine cornmeal, flour, sugar, baking powder and salt in a large bowl. Add eggs and milk. Stir to make a smooth batter; stir in bacon drippings.

(continued)

2 Pour into two greased 8x8x2-inch baking pans.
3 Bake in hot oven (450°) 25 minutes, or until crusty and golden brown. Cool slightly in pans on wire racks; serve warm.

Bridie's Irish Soda Bread

This bread is usually served at high teas and other important occasions

Bake at 400° for 40 minutes.
Makes 1 round loaf.

4 cups sifted all-purpose flour
1 tablespoon sugar
1½ teaspoons salt
1 teaspoon baking soda
1 cup dried currants
1½ cups buttermilk

1 Sift flour, sugar, salt and baking soda into a large bowl; stir in currants to coat with flour.
2 Stir in buttermilk, just until flour is moistened. Knead dough in bowl with lightly floured hands 10 times.
3 Turn dough out onto lightly floured cookie sheet and shape into an 8-inch round. Cut a cross into the top with a floured knife.
4 Bake in hot oven (400°) 40 minutes, or until loaf turns golden and sounds hollow when tapped. Cool completely on a wire rack before slicing.

At your next tailgate party, take along this southern cowboy special, **Chuckwagon Pecan Bread.**

a large bowl; stir in chopped pecans and lemon rind.
3 Beat eggs well with milk in a small bowl; stir in oil. Add all at once to flour mixture; stir just until evenly moist. Turn into prepared pan; spread top even. Press pecan halves down center of batter to decorate.
4 Bake in slow oven (325°) 1 hour and 20 minutes, or until a wooden pick inserted in center comes out clean. Cool in pan on a wire rack 10 minutes. Loosen around edges with a knife; turn out onto rack. Place right side up. Cool completely.
5 Wrap loaf in waxed paper, foil, or transparent wrap. Store overnight to mellow flavors and make slicing easier. Cut into thin slices.

Chuckwagon Pecan Bread

An up-to-date version of the cowboys' favorite

Bake at 325° for 1 hour and 20 minutes.
Makes one 8x4x2-inch loaf.

3 cups sifted all-purpose flour
1 cup sugar
4 teaspoons baking powder
1 teaspoon salt
1 cup very finely chopped pecans
2 teaspoons grated lemon rind
2 eggs
1 cup milk
¼ cup vegetable oil
Pecan halves

1 Grease an 8x4x2-inch loaf pan.
2 Sift flour, sugar, baking powder, and salt into

Basic Irish Soda Bread

Sugary syrup lightly "frosts" this fruity bread during last few minutes of baking

Bake at 375° for 55 minutes.
Makes 1 round loaf

3 cups sifted all-purpose flour
3 tablespoons sugar (for dough)
3 teaspoons baking powder
½ teaspoon baking soda
½ teaspoon salt
1 cup dried currants
1⅓ cups buttermilk
2 tablespoons sugar (for glaze)
2 tablespoons hot water

1 Sift flour, 3 tablespoons sugar, baking powder, soda, and salt into medium-size bowl;

stir in currants, then buttermilk until blended. (Dough will be sticky.)

2 Turn out onto lightly floured pastry cloth or board; knead about 10 times. Shape into an 8-inch round loaf; place on ungreased cooky sheet. Cut a cross in top of dough with sharp knife.

3 Bake in moderate oven (375°). 45 minutes; remove from oven.

4 Dissolve 2 tablespoons sugar in hot water in a cup; brush generously over hot loaf. Bake 10 minutes longer, or until richly golden. Serve warm.

QUICK BREAD TIPS

It's a good idea to bake any tea loaf the day before you plan to serve it. The flavors improve with overnight standing and loaves are easier to slice the next day. After your loaf has cooled completely, store it in an airtight container.

• Because of the consistency of loaf breads, it's best to test them for doneness by inserting a wooden pick in the center of the loaf. If the wooden pick comes out clean, the bread is done; if not, bake an additional 5 minutes and check again.

Golden Cheese Bread

Whole-wheat cereal blends with cheese in this mellow quick bread. If you have any left over, toast for breakfast

Bake at 400° for 30 minutes.
Makes 1 loaf

1¼ cups sifted all-purpose flour
2 tablespoons sugar
3 teaspoons baking powder
½ teaspoon salt
¾ cup uncooked granulated instant whole-wheat cereal
1 cup grated Cheddar cheese (4 ounces)
1 egg
¾ cup milk
¼ cup vegetable oil

1 Sift flour, sugar, baking powder, and salt into a medium-size bowl; stir in cereal and cheese.

2 Beat egg with milk and vegetable oil in a small bowl; add all at once to flour mixture, stirring just until blended. Pour into a greased loaf pan, 9x5x3.

3 Bake in hot oven (400°) 30 minutes, or until

golden and a wooden pick inserted in middle comes out clean. Cool 5 minutes on a wire rack, then turn out. Slice and serve while still warm.

Cheese Cranberry Bread

This bread is particularly popular at holiday time

Bake at 350° for 1 hour and 15 minutes.
Makes 1 loaf.

2 cups fresh or frozen cranberries
2 cups all-purpose flour
1 cup sugar
1 tablespoon baking powder
½ teaspoon salt
1½ cups shredded Cheddar cheese (6 ounces)
½ cup coarsely chopped walnuts
1 cup milk
1 egg, slightly beaten
¼ cup (½ stick) butter or margarine, melted
1 tablespoon grated orange rind

1 Halve the cranberries; set aside for Step 2.

2 Sift flour, sugar, baking powder and salt in a bowl. Add berries, cheese and nuts; toss.

3 Combine milk, egg, butter or margarine and orange rind; add to flour mixture all at once. Stir only until all dry ingredients are moistened. Turn into buttered loaf pan (9x5x2¾).

4 Bake in moderate oven (350°) 1 hour and 15 minutes, or until pick inserted in middle comes out clean. Allow to stand 10 minutes. Turn out of pan onto wire rack to cool.

Cottage Cheese Fruit Bread

A quick bread that's delicious for breakfast

Bake at 350° for 50 to 60 minutes.
Makes 2 medium-size loaves or 1 large loaf.

6 tablespoons (¾ stick) butter or margarine, softened
½ cup firmly packed light brown sugar
2 eggs
1 tablespoon grated lemon rind
1 tablespoon grated orange rind
1½ cups cottage cheese
2 cups all-purpose flour
2 teaspoons baking powder
¾ teaspoon baking soda
¾ teaspoon salt
1 cup finely chopped dried apricots
½ cup chopped pecans

(continued)

1 Cream butter in a large mixing bowl; add sugar gradually, beating well until light and fluffy. Add eggs, one at a time, beating well after each addition. Add fruit rinds and cottage cheese; beat.

2 Mix flour, baking powder, soda and salt; add to butter-egg mixture. Mix just until blended. Fold in apricots and nuts. Turn into two buttered (7⅜x3⅝x2¼-inch) loaf pans or one (9x5x3-inch) loaf pan.

3 Bake in a moderate oven (350°) for 50 minutes for medium-size loaves, and 1 hour for large loaf, or until cake tester inserted in middle comes out clean. Turn loaves onto wire rack to cool.

Cheddar Cheese Bread

Make this in miniature-size loaves for serving with appetizers, or large ones for gift-giving

Bake at 350° for 45 minutes for large loaf,
35 minutes for small.
Makes 1 large whole wheat loaf
or 6 miniature ones.

1¼ cups sifted all-purpose flour
½ cup sugar
1 teaspoon baking powder
1 teaspoon baking soda
1 teaspoon salt
2 cups shredded Cheddar cheese (8 ounces)
1¼ cups whole wheat flour
1 cup chopped nuts
1 tablespoon grated orange rind
1 egg, slightly beaten
1¼ cups milk
¼ cup (½ stick) butter or margarine, melted
¼ cup light molasses

1 Sift together the flour, sugar, baking powder, baking soda and salt in a large bowl; add cheese, whole wheat flour, nuts and orange rind; blend all the ingredients thoroughly.

2 Combine egg, milk, butter and molasses; add all at once to sifted dry ingredients and stir only until blended. Spread evenly in large (9¼x5¼x2¾-inch) loaf pan or 6 miniature-size loaf pans.

3 Bake in moderate oven (350°) 45 minutes for large loaf and 35 minutes for miniature loaves, or until cake tester inserted in center comes out clean. Allow to stand for 5 minutes; remove from pan onto wire rack to cool.

Variation: 1¼ cups sifted all-purpose flour may be substituted for the whole wheat flour.

Turkish Fruit Strudel

Pearl Fried, a native of Turkey, shares her recipe for a quick-to-make pastry delight

Bake at 325° for 40 minutes.
Makes 4 loaves.

4 cups all purpose flour
1 tablespoon baking powder
½ teaspoon salt
3 eggs
½ cup vegetable oil
1 cup sugar
1 tablespoon vanilla
1 jar (16 ounces) prune lekvar*
1 cup raisins
1 cup chopped walnuts
¼ cup sugar
2 teaspoons ground cinnamon

1 Sift flour, baking powder and salt onto wax paper. Beat eggs until fluffy in a large bowl with a wire whip. Measure 2 tablespoons into a cup and reserve.

2 Beat vegetable oil, the 1 cup sugar and vanilla into remaining eggs until well blended with a wire whip. Work in flour mixture to make a soft dough.

3 Roll out dough, one quarter at a time, to a 14x10-inch rectangle on a lightly floured pastry cloth; spread dough with ¼ of the lekvar; sprinkle with ¼ of the raisins and chopped nuts; roll up, jelly-roll fashion, starting at a short end and using the pastry cloth to help lift the dough. Place, seam-side down, on a large cookie sheet.

4 Repeat with remaining dough and filling to make 4 rolls. Brush reserved beaten egg over loaves. Combine the ¼ cup sugar and cinnamon in a cup; sprinkle over loaves.

5 Bake in slow oven (325°) for 40 minutes, or until loaves are a golden brown; cool on cookie sheets on wire racks 10 minutes; slide off sheets onto wire racks; cool completely. Wrap and freeze.

*Prune Lekvar is a very thick prune butter that is sold in Middle European and Middle Eastern specialty shops. If you can't find it, make your own by pitting and cooking 1 pound prunes with 1 cup sugar and ½ cup water until very thick; cool 15 minutes; process on high speed in electric blender until smooth. Cool completely before using. Spread ⅓ cup of mixture for each loaf.

Aprikosenflek

Make a batch of them when apricots are in season, then freeze for delicious winter eating

Bake at 350° for 1 hour.
Makes one 9-inch round
or one 13x9x2-inch cake.

4 eggs, separated
1¼ cups sugar
1¼ cups (2½ sticks) butter or margarine
    Rind of 1 lemon, grated
2 cups all purpose flour
½ teaspoon salt
1 pound ripe apricots, halved and pitted

1 Beat egg whites until foamy and double in volume in small bowl of electric mixer at high speed. Gradually beat in ¼ cup of the sugar to make a soft meringue.
2 Beat butter or margarine and remaining 1 cup sugar until light and fluffy in large bowl of electric mixer at high speed. Beat in egg yolks, one at a time, until well blended; stir in lemon rind.
3 Fold in egg whites with a wire whip until well blended. Gradually stir in flour and salt, just until smooth.
4 Spread batter into a buttered 9-inch quiche/flan pan or a 13x9x2-inch baking pan. Arrange apricots, rounded side up, on top of batter; sprinkle with sugar.
5 Bake in moderate oven (350°) 1 hour, or until a wooden pick inserted into center comes out clean. Cool in pan on wire rack 10 minutes; loosen cake around edge and remove from pan. Cool completely; wrap and freeze.
To serve: Loosen foil around cake and heat in moderate oven (350°) for 20 minutes. Garnish with a ring of red maraschino cherries.

BISCUITS AND MUFFINS

Popovers

Giant airy puffs with hot crispy shells—butter them and eat right away

Bake at 400° F. for 50 minutes.
Makes 8 large popovers.

2 eggs
1 cup milk
1 cup sifted all-purpose flour
½ teaspoon salt

1 Heat oven to 400° F. Heavily butter 8 six-ounce custard cups; place on baking sheet for easy handling; slide into hot oven to heat while mixing batter.
2 Beat eggs slightly in bowl or 1-quart measure; add remaining ingredients; beat briskly ½ minute; scrape beater and sides of bowl; beat ½ minute longer. Batter will be creamy-smooth and rather thin.
3 Pour into heated custard cups, filling each ⅓ full to allow room for popping.
4 Bake in hot oven (400° F.) 50 minutes, or until popped, crisp, and golden-brown. *Do not peek during baking, for they may fall.* Serve hot with butter or margarine and jam.

BISCUIT VARIATIONS

Drop Biscuits: Prepare BAKING POWDER BISCUITS *increasing the milk to 1 cup. Drop by spoonfuls, 1 inch apart on ungreased cooky sheet. Bake following biscuit directions.*

Sesame Butter Fingers: *Turn oven to hot (450°). Melt ¼ cup butter or margarine in a 9x9x2-inch pan. Put ½ cup sesame seeds on a large plate. Prepare* BAKING POWDER BISCUITS. *Roll or pat dough to an 8-inch square on a lightly floured surface. Cut square in half. Cut each half into nine 4-inch strips. Dip each strip into the melted butter, then dip one side into sesame seeds. Arrange strips in 2 rows in the baking pan. Bake 15 minutes or until golden brown.*

Scones: *Prepare* BAKING POWDER BISCUITS *recipe, but do not add milk. Add 3 tablespoons sugar, 1 teaspoon grated orange rind and ½ cup raisins to dry mix. Beat 1 egg with ⅓ cup milk; pour into dry ingredients. Stir and knead as in biscuits. Divide dough in half. Pat each half to an 8-inch circle. Cut each circle into 6 wedges. Brush tops with milk; sprinkle with sugar. Place wedges, 1 inch apart on ungreased cookie sheet. Bake in a very hot oven (450°) 10 minutes or until golden brown.*

Baking Powder Biscuits

Flaky, light buttered biscuits to serve with Sunday dinner: or try one of our biscuit variations, for a tea-time snack

Bake at 450° for 12 minutes.
Makes 12 biscuits.

2 cups sifted all-purpose flour
3 teaspoons baking powder
½ teaspoon salt
¼ cup vegetable shortening
¾ cup milk

1 Sift flour, baking powder and salt into a large bowl.
2 Cut in shortening with a pastry blender until mixture resembles cornmeal.
3 Add milk; stir lightly with a fork until a soft puffy dough forms.
4 Turn out onto a lightly floured surface. Knead lightly about 20 turns.
5 Roll or pat dough to a ½-inch thickness. Cut into 2-inch rounds with a floured biscuit cutter, working neatly from rim to middle so there will be few scraps to reroll. Place biscuits on an ungreased cookie sheet 1 inch apart.
6 Bake in a hot oven (450°) 12 minutes or until golden brown.

Yorkshire Pudding

Use them with roast beef or, as the British do, with jelly

Bake at 450° for 15 minutes.
Makes 12 puddings.

2 tablespoons roast beef drippings
POPOVER batter (see index for recipe)

Spoon 2 tablespoons of roast beef pan drippings into each of two 8x1½-inch round layer pans. Place in oven as it heats to 450°. Divide POPOVER batter between the two pans. Bake in a very hot oven (450°) 15 minutes. Lower temperature to 350°; bake 20 minutes longer or until puddings are puffed and brown.

When you have a few extra minutes in the morning, cook these **Baking Powder Biscuits.** One bite, and you'll be glad you took the time.

Basic Muffins

Melt-in-the-mouth biscuits—delicious plain or with cheese or bacon

Bake at 400° for 25 minutes.
Makes 12 medium-size muffins.

2 cups sifted all-purpose flour
2 tablespoons sugar
2 teaspoons baking powder
1 teaspoon salt
1 egg, beaten
1 cup milk
¼ cup melted butter or margarine

1 Sift flour, sugar, baking powder and salt into a medium-size bowl. Make a well in center of ingredients.
2 Combine egg, milk and melted butter or margarine in a small bowl; add all at once to flour mixture; stir lightly just until liquid is absorbed. (Batter will be lumpy.)
3 Spoon into 12 greased medium-size muffin-pan cups to fill ⅔ full.
4 Bake in a hot oven (400°) 25 minutes or until touched with brown and springy to the touch. Serve hot.

Apple Streusel Muffins

Mouth-watering muffins chock full of apples and sprinkled with walnuts for the perfect topping

Bake at 425° for 20 minutes.
Makes 12 muffins.

2 cups sifted all-purpose flour
½ cup sugar (for batter)
3 teaspoons baking powder
1 teaspoon salt
½ cup (1 stick) butter or margarine
1 medium-size tart apple, pared, quartered, cored, and diced (1 cup)
2 teaspoons grated lemon rind
1 egg
⅔ cup milk
¼ cup walnuts, chopped
2 tablespoons sugar (for topping)

1 Sift flour, the ½ cup sugar, baking powder and salt into a large bowl. Cut in butter or margarine with a pastry blender until mixture is crumbly. Measure out ½ cup for topping; reserve. Stir apple and 1 teaspoon of the lemon rind into mixture in bowl.
2 Beat eggs in a small bowl; stir in milk. Add all at once to apple mixture; stir lightly just until moist. (Batter will be lumpy.) Spoon into 12 greased medium-size muffin-pan cups, filling each ⅔ full.
3 Blend reserved crumb mixture with remaining lemon rind, walnuts, and the 2 tablespoons of sugar; sprinkle over batter in each cup.
4 Bake in a hot oven (425°) 20 minutes, or until golden and tops spring back when pressed with fingertip. Remove from cups to a wire rack. Serve warm with butter or margarine and jelly, if you wish.

Blueberry Muffins

Come berry season, use fresh blueberries instead of the frozen variety called for here

Bake at 425° for 20 minutes.
Makes 12 medium-size muffins.

2 cups sifted all-purpose flour
⅓ cup sugar (for batter)
3 teaspoons baking powder
1 teaspoon salt
1 egg, well beaten
1 cup milk

¼ cup (½ stick) butter or margarine, melted and cooled
1 cup frozen quick-thaw blueberries, drained (from a 10-ounce package)
1 tablespoon sugar (for topping)
1 teaspoon grated lemon rind

1 Sift flour, the ⅓ cup sugar, baking powder and salt into a large bowl. Mix egg, milk and melted, cooled butter or margarine in a small bowl; add all at once to flour mixture; stir lightly with a fork just until liquid is absorbed. (Batter will be lumpy.) Fold in blueberries.
2 Spoon into greased medium-size muffin-pan cups, filling each ⅔ full. Sprinkle with a mixture of the 1 tablespoon sugar and lemon rind.
3 Bake in a hot oven (425°) 20 minutes, or until golden; remove from pans. Serve hot.

MUFFIN VARIATIONS

Jelly Muffins: Spoon part of batter into cups; add a dab of jelly; top with remaining batter.

Cheese Muffins: Add ½ cup shredded Cheddar cheese to dry ingredients.

Bacon Muffins: Add 4 slices of crumbled, crisp-cooked bacon to dry ingredients.

Wheat Germ Muffins

Doubly rich with old-fashioned molasses and nut-sweet wheat germ—and good for you, too

Bake at 400° for 30 minutes.
Makes 12 medium-size muffins

1½ cups sifted all-purpose flour
¼ cup sugar
2 teaspoons baking powder
1 teaspoon salt
1 cup wheat germ (from a 12-ounce jar)
1 egg, well beaten
¾ cup milk
4 tablespoons (½ stick) butter or margarine, melted
¼ cup molasses

1 Sift flour, sugar, baking powder, and salt into medium-size bowl; stir in wheat germ.
2 Combine egg, milk, melted butter or margarine, and molasses in small bowl; add all at once

(continued)

PROFESSIONAL MUFFIN SECRETS

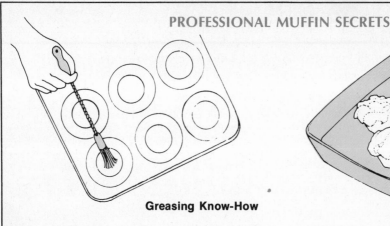

Greasing Know-How

Magic Oven

Melt shortening in each muffin cup (or use vegetable oil) and swish with a pastry brush. Or rub cups with the inside of a butter or margarine wrapper or a piece of buttered bread

Call on your electric skillet to freshen just a few muffins. The musts are a snug cover and low heat. Allow from 10 to 20 minutes, depending on size and quantity

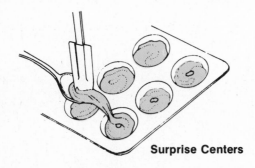

Surprise Centers

Keeping Them Warm

Next time you make plain muffins, hide a surprise in the center. Spoon part of batter into cups; add a dab of jelly or a cheese cube; top with remaining batter

If muffins are done ahead of serving time, loosen them from their cups, tilt slightly, then slide the pan back into the oven to stay warm. This keeps the muffins from steaming on the bottom.

Cut Cleanup

Made-to-Order Bakers

Not enough batter to fill your muffin pan? Pour some water into the empty cups or wipe out the grease so it doesn't scorch or turn the pan brown

Out of muffin pans? Bring out your metal jar rings—the kind used for canning—and place them on a cooky sheet. Set a paper baking cup in each; half-fill with batter and bake as usual. Or use your custard cups

to flour mixture; stir lightly just until liquid is absorbed. (Batter will be lumpy.)

3 Spoon into 12 greased medium-size muffin-pan cups to fill ⅔ full.

4 Bake in hot oven (400°) 30 minutes, or until richly browned; remove from pan at once; serve hot with butter or margarine and your favorite jelly, jam, marmalade, or preserves.

Whole Wheat Muffins

Vitamin-rich whole wheat make these zesty morning muffins a nutritious boost

Bake at 400° for 25 minutes.
Makes 12 medium-size muffins.

1 cup sifted all-purpose flour
2 teaspoons baking powder
1 teaspoon salt
1 cup unsifted whole wheat flour
¼ cup molasses
1 egg, beaten
1 cup milk
¼ cup melted butter or margarine

1 Sift all-purpose flour, baking powder and salt into a medium-size bowl; stir in whole wheat flour and make a well in center of ingredients.

2 Combine molasses, egg, milk and melted butter or margarine in a small bowl; add all at once to flour mixture; stir lightly just until liquid is absorbed. (Batter will be lumpy.)

3 Spoon into 12 greased medium-sized muffin-pan cups to fill ⅔ full.

4 Bake in a hot oven (400°) 25 minutes or until golden brown and springy to the touch. Serve hot.

Corn Muffins

Buttermilk plus cornmeal make these sunny "wake-up" muffins good to accompany bacon and eggs

Bake at 400° for 20 minutes.
Makes 12 medium-size muffins.

1 cup sifted all-purpose flour
3 tablespoons sugar

1½ teaspoons baking powder
½ teaspoon baking soda
½ teaspoon salt
1 cup yellow or white corn meal
1 egg, well beaten
⅔ cup buttermilk
¼ cup vegetable shortening, melted

1 Sift flour, sugar, baking powder, soda, and salt into a large bowl; stir in corn meal.

2 Mix egg and buttermilk in a 1-cup measure; add all at once to flour mixture; stir lightly with a fork just until liquid is absorbed; stir in melted shortening.

3 Spoon into greased medium-size muffin-pan cups, filling each ⅔ full.

4 Bake in hot oven (400°) 20 minutes, or until golden. Serve hot.

Bran Muffins

For a nutritional plus, serve these bran and molasses treats with a brunch

Bake at 400° for 20 minutes.
Makes 12 medium-size muffins.

2¼ cups whole bran
1 cup buttermilk
⅓ cup molasses
¼ cup firmly packed brown sugar
1 cup sifted all-purpose flour
1 teaspoon baking powder
1 teaspoon baking soda
1 teaspoon salt
1 egg, slightly beaten
¼ cup vegetable shortening, melted

1 Mix bran, buttermilk, molasses, and brown sugar in a small bowl; let stand until liquid is absorbed.

2 Sift flour, baking powder, soda, and salt into a large bowl.

3 Stir egg and melted shortening into bran mixture. Add all at once to flour mixture; stir lightly with a fork just until evenly moist. Spoon into greased medium-size muffin-pan cups, filling each ⅔ full.

4 Bake in hot oven (400°) 20 minutes, or until richly golden. Serve hot.

PANCAKES AND WAFFLES

Pancakes

Quick-as-a-flash pancakes, topped with maple syrup

Makes 6 servings.

2 cups sifted all-purpose flour
3 teaspoons baking powder
1 tablespoon sugar
2 eggs, well beaten
1½ cups milk
2 tablespoons vegetable oil or melted vegetable shortening

1 Sift flour, baking powder and sugar onto a piece of wax paper.
2 Combine eggs and milk in a medium-size mixing bowl.
3 Add sifted dry ingredients to the egg-milk mixture and beat until smooth; stir in vegetable oil or melted shortening.
4 Bake on a medium hot griddle and serve immediately.

Buttermilk Griddle Cakes

Loved by the legendary cowboys—accompany with molasses syrup or spoon chilled fruits over

Makes 6 servings.

2 cups sifted all-purpose flour
1 teaspoon baking soda
1 teaspoon salt
1 tablespoon sugar
2 eggs, well beaten
2 cups buttermilk
2 tablespoons vegetable oil or melted vegetable shortening

1 Sift flour, baking soda, salt and sugar onto a piece of wax paper.
2 Combine eggs and buttermilk in a medium-size mixing bowl.
3 Add sifted dry ingredients to the buttermilk mixture and beat until smooth; stir in vegetable oil or melted shortening.
4 Bake on a medium hot griddle and serve immediately.

Breakfast on the road or breakfast at home, **Pancakes** and maple syrup are all-American favorites.

HOW TO MAKE PERFECT PANCAKES

1 Make sure griddle is just-right hot before adding the batter. Here's how to test it: Sprinkle on several drops of water; when they sputter and dance about, grease griddle and start pouring.

2 For even-size pancakes, measure batter, using a scant quarter cup for a 4-inch round. The batter spreads, so leave a little space between cakes and they will keep their shape and be easy to turn.

3 When pancakes look puffy and slightly dry around edge, bubbles cover the top, and the underside is golden, flip them over with a wide spatula. Bake a few minutes more, or until bottoms brown.

4 If pancakes must stand before serving, keep them hot this undercover way. Place in a pie plate, turn a colander upside-down over top, and set in a warm place. Heat stays in, steam wafts out.

Waffles

What better breakfast than golden waffles topped with syrup

Makes 6 waffles.

> 2 *cups sifted all-purpose flour*
> 2 *teaspoons baking powder*
> ½ *teaspoon salt*
> 3 *tablespoons sugar*
> 2 *eggs, separated*
> 1¼ *cups milk*
> 6 *tablespoons vegetable oil or melted vegetable shortening*

1 Sift flour with baking powder, salt and sugar onto a large piece of wax paper.
2 Beat egg whites until stiff but not dry; set aside.
3 Beat egg yolks well in a medium-size bowl and stir in milk.
4 Add sifted dry ingredients and mix just enough to blend; add vegetable oil or melted shortening. Fold in egg whites.
5 Bake in a moderately hot waffle iron 4 to 5 minutes until crisp and brown or as iron manufacturer directs. Serve hot with melted butter and syrup or honey.

Waffle Whip-Ups

Children adore them—crispy, buttered, smothered in molasses syrup, or covered with fruits

Makes 4 servings

> 3 *cups sifted all-purpose flour*
> 3 *tablespoons sugar*
> 4 *teaspoons baking powder*
> 1 *teaspoon salt*
> 3 *eggs, separated*
> 2¼ *cups milk*
> ½ *cup butter or margarine, melted*
> BUTTERSCOTCH TOPPING *(recipe follows)*
> PEACH-COCONUT TOPPING *(recipe follows)*

1 Sift flour, sugar, baking powder and salt onto wax paper.
2 Beat egg whites just until they stand in firm peaks in a small bowl.
3 Beat egg yolks until thick and lemon-colored in large bowl; stir in milk and melted butter or margarine.
4 Sift dry ingredients into egg yolk mixture, stirring just until batter is smooth. Fold in beaten egg whites until no streaks of white remain.
5 Bake (using 1⅓ cups batter for each waffle) in waffle iron, following manufacturer's directions.
6 Serve with your choice of toppings.

Butterscotch Topping

Makes 3 cups

> 2 *cups (two 6-ounce packages) butterscotch pieces*
> ¼ *cup (½ stick) butter or margarine*
> ¾ *cup water*
> 4 *cups miniature marshmallows*
> ⅛ *teaspoon ground allspice*

1 Combine butterscotch pieces, butter or margarine, and water in medium-size saucepan. Cook over low heat, stirring constantly, until butterscotch is melted.
2 Gradually add marshmallows, stirring until melted. Add allspice; mix well. Serve warm.

Convenience foods and convenient hurry-up kitchen equipment make cooking hot waffles a snap.

Peach-Coconut Topping

Makes 2 cups.

1 can (1 pound) sliced cling peaches
¼ cup sugar
2 teaspoons cornstarch
½ cup flaked coconut

1 Drain peach syrup into a 1-cup measure; add water, if necessary, to make 1 cup liquid; reserve. Chop peaches.
2 Combine sugar and cornstarch in medium-size saucepan; add reserved liquid; mix well. Cook, stirring constantly, until sauce thickens and boils 1 minute.
3 Add peaches; simmer 10 minutes; remove from heat. Stir in coconut; cool; chill.

FRITTERS AND FRIED BREAD

Fry Bread

Sometimes called sopaipillas. As they cook, they puff blistery golden. Serve them hot as the bread of the meal

Makes 32 pieces

2 cups sifted all-purpose flour
2 teaspoons baking powder
1 teaspoon salt
1 egg
3 tablespoons vegetable oil
½ cup water
Shortening or vegetable oil for frying

1 Sift flour, baking powder, and salt into a medium-size bowl.
2 Beat egg in a small bowl; stir in vegetable oil and water. Pour over dry ingredients, stirring with a fork until well-blended.
3 Turn out onto a lightly floured pastry cloth or board; knead until smooth; divide dough in half. Roll out each to a 12-inch square, then cut into 16 three-inch squares.
4 Melt enough shortening or pour in enough vegetable oil to make a 2-inch depth in an electric deep-fat fryer or deep heavy saucepan; heat to 380°.
5 Fry squares, 2 or 3 at a time and turning often, 3 to 4 minutes, or until puffed and golden. Lift out with a slotted spoon; drain on paper toweling; keep warm.

Corn Fritters

Excellent go-alongs with ham and eggs

Makes about 1 dozen.

1 cup sifted all-purpose flour
1 teaspoon baking powder
1 teaspoon sugar
½ teaspoon salt
2 eggs, well beaten
½ cup milk
1 teaspoon vegetable oil
1 cup cooked or canned whole kernel corn, well drained
Vegetable oil or vegetable shortening for deep fat frying

1 Sift flour, baking powder, sugar and salt onto a piece of wax paper.
2 Combine eggs and milk in a medium-size mixing bowl; add sifted dry ingredients and beat lightly to mix; stir in 1 teaspoon vegetable oil and the corn.
3 Drop from a tablespoon into deep hot fat (375°) and fry until golden brown on all sides. Drain on paper toweling and serve at once.

Chapati

Similar to a Mexican tortilla, serve this Indian pancake with curries

Makes 16 six-inch wafers.

2 cups sifted all-purpose flour
1 teaspoon salt
¾ cup water
Vegetable shortening or vegetable oil for frying

1 Combine flour and salt in a medium-size bowl. Stir in water until all flour is moist and dough is stiff and evenly blended.
2 Turn out onto a lightly floured pastry cloth or board; knead 5 minutes, or until dough is smooth.
3 Roll out on cloth or board with palms of hands to form a long log; cut into 16 even pieces. Let stand 15 minutes.
4 Roll each piece to a 6-inch round with a rolling pin. (Dough will be very thin.)
5 Melt enough vegetable shortening or pour vegetable oil into a deep-fat fryer or heavy large saucepan to fill two thirds full; heat to 390°.
6 Fry rounds, one at a time, turning once, several minutes, or until golden. (Bubbles of varying sizes will form all over dough as it cooks.) Lift out with a slotted spoon; drain on paper toweling. Serve warm or cold.

Two fruit-jeweled sweet breads, one **Petaled Honey Ring,** background to put together in a jiffy using commercial refrigerated dinner rolls, the other **Almond Foldovers,** (see index for recipe) to make from scratch, knead, shape and bake.

Convenience Bread Fix-Ups

Get a head start on bread baking by first using one of the many convenience ingredients at hand. Whether it is a roll-mix, a gingerbread or muffin mix, or one of the other mixes in your market they will make your first entry into this exciting part of cookery easy and quick.

Sunburst

With hot-roll mix, you can fix this large coffee cake in 20 minutes

Bake at 350° for 20 minutes.
Makes 1 large coffee cake.

 1 *package (13¾ ounces) hot-roll mix*
10 *tablespoons sugar*
 2 *tablespoons vegetable shortening*
 2 *eggs*
 ¾ *cup warm water*
 1 *envelope (1 ounce) liquid unsweetened chocolate*
 1 *teaspoon ground cinnamon*
 3 *tablespoons butter or margarine, softened*
 ½ *cup chopped walnuts*

1 Combine hot-roll mix, 2 tablespoons of the sugar, and shortening in a large bowl; prepare with 1 of the eggs and water, following label directions. Cover with a clean towel. Let rise in a warm place, away from draft, 1 hour, or until double in bulk.
2 While dough rises, blend chocolate, remaining 8 tablespoons sugar, cinnamon, and butter or margarine in a small bowl.
3 Punch dough down; turn out onto a lightly floured pastry cloth or board. Knead 50 times, or until smooth; cover again; let stand 10 minutes.
4 Roll out dough to a rectangle, 20x10; spread chocolate mixture evenly over top; sprinkle ¼ cup of the walnuts over chocolate layer. Cut rectangle in half lengthwise; starting at a long side, roll up each half tightly, jelly-roll fashion.
5 Cut one roll into 6 equal pieces; cut 4 pieces, the same size, from second roll. Twist remaining piece into a coil and place in center of a lightly greased large cooky sheet. Pinch ends of all pieces to seal, then arrange around coil to form a sunburst design.

6 Beat remaining egg slightly in a small bowl; brush all over dough. Sprinkle remaining ¼ cup walnuts over top; cover.
7 Let rise again in a warm place, away from draft, 45 minutes, or until double in bulk.
8 Bake in moderate oven (350°) 20 minutes, or until golden and loaf gives a hollow sound when tapped. Remove from cooky sheet to a wire rack. Serve warm or cold.

Arkansas Jalapena Cornbread

Jalapena peppers are the hot green peppers you buy in a can: be sure to scrape out all the seeds before chopping, or your bread will be bitter

Bake at 400° for 35 minutes.
Makes three 9-inch rounds.

 2 *packages (8 ounces each) corn muffin mix*
 2 *cups milk*
 ½ *cup vegetable oil*
 3 *eggs, beaten*
 1 *large onion, grated*
 2 *tablespoons sugar*
 1 *can (8 ounces) cream-style corn*
 ½ *cup seeded and chopped Jalapena (hot green) peppers*
1½ *cups shredded Cheddar cheese (6 ounces)*
 ¼ *cup chopped and drained pimiento*

1 Combine corn muffin mix, milk, vegetable oil, eggs, onion, sugar, cream-style corn, Jalapena peppers, Cheddar cheese and pimiento in a large bowl; mix just until blended with a wooden spoon.
2 Divide batter among 3 greased 9-inch layer-cake pans.
3 Bake in hot oven (400°) 35 minutes, or until breads are golden. Cool in pans 5 minutes; invert onto wire racks, then turn top-side up immediately. Cool completely.

Petaled Honey Ring

Sweet bread for the coffee break or an afternoon treat

Bake at 350° for 25 minutes.
Makes 1 nine-inch ring.

2 packages (8 ounces each) refrigerated butterflake dinner rolls
3 tablespoons currants
3 teaspoons grated lemon rind
3 tablespoons honey
4 tablespoons (½ stick) butter or margarine, melted

1 Separate each package of rolls to make 24 even pieces. Place 12 pieces in a well-buttered 7-cup ring mold to make an even layer. Sprinkle 1 tablespoon of the currants and 1 teaspoon of the lemon rind over layer, then drizzle 1 tablespoon each of the honey and melted butter or margarine over top.
2 Make two more layers the same way; place remaining rolls on top. Drizzle remaining butter or margarine over all.
3 Bake in moderate oven (350°) 25 minutes, or until firm and golden. Loosen at once around edge with knife; invert onto a serving plate. Let stand 10 minutes. To serve, pull off layers with two forks; serve warm.

Cheese 'n' Bacon Corn Bread

Cut this savory bread into squares and serve hot right from its pan

Bake at 400° for 25 minutes.
Makes 1 loaf

1 package corn muffin mix
½ cup shredded sharp Cheddar cheese
6 slices bacon, cooked and crumbled
1 egg
    Milk

1 Empty corn muffin mix into a medium-size bowl. Save about 1 tablespoon each cheese and bacon for topping; stir remaining into muffin mix.
2 Mix in egg and milk, following label directions; pour into greased baking pan, 8x8x2.
3 Bake in hot oven (400°) 15 minutes; sprinkle saved cheese and bacon on top; bake 10 minutes longer, or until firm and richly golden.

Spoon Bread

Grits, ham, eggs, and spoon bread, or spoon bread and jelly—either way it's delicious

Bake at 325° for 1 hour and 25 minutes.
Makes 6 servings.

3 eggs
2 cups milk
2 tablespoons butter or margarine, melted
1 package corn-bread mix

1 Beat eggs well in a medium-size bowl; beat in milk, butter or margarine and corn-bread mix until smooth with a rotary beater. Pour into a greased 6-cup baking dish.
2 Bake in slow oven (325°) 1 hour and 25 minutes, or until firm and golden.
3 Serve at once in place of potatoes with butter or margarine or gravy.

Golden Herb-Cheese Bread

A breakfast loaf that is equally as good as a suppertime treat

Bake at 375° for 40 to 45 minutes.
Makes 1 loaf.

¼ cup grated Parmesan cheese
¼ cup minced parsley
¼ teaspoon leaf basil, crumbled
¼ teaspoon leaf oregano, crumbled
1 package hot-roll mix
    Yellow cornmeal
2 tablespoons melted butter or margarine

1 Stir cheese, parsley and herbs into hot-roll mix; make into dough, following label directions for bread; knead; let rise; knead again; shape into loaf, following label directions.
2 Place in loaf pan, 9x5x2½, greased and sprinkled lightly with cornmeal; let rise until double in bulk; make gashes across top 1½ inches deep; brush with melted butter or margarine; sprinkle with more cornmeal.
3 Bake in moderate oven (375°) 40 to 45 minutes, or until firm.

Orange-Walnut Bread

So rich in flavor—just right to accompany the afternoon beverage

Bake at 350° for 55 minutes.
Makes 1 loaf, 8x4x2.

1 package (14 ounces) orange muffin mix
Egg
Milk
¾ cup chopped walnuts
2 tablespoons sugar
½ teaspoon ground cinnamon
1 tablespoon butter or margarine, melted

1 Prepare muffin mix with egg and milk, following label directions; stir in ½ cup of the walnuts. Spoon into a greased loaf pan, 8x4x2.
2 Mix sugar, cinnamon, melted butter or margarine and remaining ¼ cup walnuts in a small bowl; sprinkle evenly over batter.
3 Bake in moderate oven (350°) 55 minutes, or until golden and a wooden pick inserted in center comes out clean. Cool in pan on a wire rack 10 minutes. Loosen around edges with a knife; turn out onto rack. Sprinkle with grated lemon peel, if you wish; let loaf cool completely.
4 Wrap in wax paper, foil or transparent wrap. Store overnight to mellow flavors and make slicing easier. Cut in thin slices.

Steamed Ginger Brown Bread

For a flavor contrast, serve with a thick, rich egg custard—or drizzle warm custard over

Makes 2 loaves.

1 package gingerbread mix
¼ cup yellow cornmeal
1 teaspoon salt
1½ cups milk
1 cup seedless raisins

1 Combine gingerbread mix, cornmeal and salt in a large bowl; stir in milk until mixture is evenly moist, then beat at medium speed of electric mixer 2 minutes; stir in raisins.
2 Pour batter into two greased 1-pound coffee cans; cover with foil; fasten with string to hold tightly.
3 Place cans on a rack or trivet in a kettle or steamer; pour in boiling water to half the depth of cans; cover.
4 Steam 3 hours, or until bread is firm and a long skewer inserted in center comes out clean. (Keep water boiling gently during entire cooking time, adding more boiling water, if needed.)
5 Cool bread in cans on a wire rack 5 minutes. Loosen around edges with a knife; turn out onto rack; cool. Slice and serve warm or cold.

Turnover Fruit Bread

A homey fruit-filled loaf, fascinatingly inviting in its shapelessness

Bake at 375° for 35 minutes.
Makes 1 loaf

1 package (13¾ ounces) hot-roll mix
¼ cup warm water
4 tablespoons (½ stick) butter or margarine
2 tablespoons sugar
1 teaspoon grated lemon rind
¼ teaspoon salt
2 eggs
Fruit Filling (recipe follows)
Butter or margarine
2 tablespoons 10X (confectioners' powdered) sugar

1 Sprinkle yeast from hot-roll mix over warm water in 1-cup measure; stir to dissolve.
2 Cream 4 tablespoons butter or margarine with granulated sugar, lemon rind, and salt in medium-size bowl. Beat in eggs until mixture is light. Stir in dissolved yeast; blend in dry ingredients from hot-roll mix.
3 Turn out onto lightly floured pastry cloth or board; knead until smooth and elastic, adding only enough flour to keep dough from sticking. Place in greased bowl; cover with clean towel; let rise in warm place, away from draft, 1 hour, or until double in bulk.
4 Punch dough down; turn out onto lightly floured pastry cloth or board; roll out to a circle about ½ inch thick; turn over (so top will bake smooth); spread with Fruit Filling to within 1 inch of edge.
5 Pull edge of dough up and over all the way around to center to cover filling completely; pinch dough together to seal. Turn loaf over and place on cooky sheet. Cover with clean towel; let rise in warm place, away from draft, 1 hour, or until double in bulk.
6 Bake in moderate oven (375°) 35 minutes, or until golden-brown; brush top with butter or margarine; cool on wire rack. Sprinkle with 10X sugar.

(continued)

FRUIT FILLING

Drain syrup from 1 can (about 8 ounces) crushed pineapple into small saucepan; add 1½ cups dried prunes. Cover; simmer 5 minutes; remove from heat and let stand 20 minutes, or until prunes are plump and syrup is absorbed. Pit prunes and cut in small pieces; stir in drained pineapple and 1 teaspoon pumpkin-pie spice, mixing well. Makes about 1½ cups.

Sugared Apricot Miniatures

Snowy snack-size loaves bake in your individual gelatin molds

> Bake at 350° for 35 minutes.
> Makes 8 small loaves

1 package (about 15 ounces) apricot-nut bread mix
½ teaspoon ground cinnamon
1 egg
1 cup pineapple juice
1 teaspoon vanilla
10X (confectioners' powdered) sugar

1 Grease 8 individual gelatin molds.
2 Combine nut-bread mix and cinnamon in a large bowl; add egg, pineapple juice and vanilla; mix, following label directions. Spoon into prepared molds, filling each about ¾ full. Set molds, not touching, in a jelly-roll pan for ease in handling.
3 Bake in moderate oven (350°) 35 minutes, or until centers spring back when lightly pressed with fingertip. Cool in molds on wire racks 10 minutes. Loosen around edges with a knife; turn out onto racks; cool completely. Sprinkle lightly with 10X sugar and garnish each with a dried apricot and walnut half, if you wish.

Cheddar Biscuits

Make a perfect breakfast even better with these munchable biscuits

> Bake at 425° for 10 minutes.
> Makes 12 biscuits.

2 cups biscuit mix
¾ cup shredded sharp Cheddar cheese

3 tablespoons bacon-flavor bits
Milk

1 Combine biscuit mix, cheese and bacon bits in a large bowl; add milk, following label directions, stirring just until mixture is moist.
2 Turn dough out onto a lightly floured pastry cloth or board; knead 8 to 10 times. Roll out ½ inch thick; cut into rounds with a 2-inch biscuit cutter. Place on a large cookie sheet.
3 Bake in hot oven (425°) 10 minutes, or until puffed and golden. Serve hot.

Cheddar Biscuits

Tucked into each quick-mix biscuit is a cube of sharp cheese. Recipe gives a slick shaping hint

> Bake at 450° for 12 minutes.
> Makes 12 biscuits

2 cups biscuit mix
Milk
12 cubes sharp Cheddar cheese (from a 6-ounce package)

1 Prepare biscuit mix with milk, following label directions for 12 biscuits. Turn out onto lightly floured pastry cloth or board; knead 8 to 10 times.
2 Roll dough out to a rectangle, 12x8; place 12 cubes of cheese, about 1½ inches apart in 3 rows of 4 each, on half of dough; fold other half over to make a second layer:
3 Cut into 12 about-2-inch squares, cutting between cubes of cheese; place on greased cooky sheet.
4 Bake in very hot oven (450°) 12 minutes, or until richly golden.

Miniature Dill Loaves

Served piping-hot, this herb-seasoned bread dresses any meal in grand style

> Bake at 375° for 30 minutes.
> Makes 3 little loaves

1 package (8 ounces) refrigerated flaky biscuits
4 tablespoons (½ stick) butter or margarine, melted
½ teaspoon dill weed

1 Separate the 12 biscuits; dip each into melted butter or margarine in a pie plate. Stand 4 each into ungreased toy-size loaf pans; sprinkle with dill weed. Place pans on a cooky sheet for easy handling, if you wish.
2 Bake in moderate oven (375°) 30 minutes, or until golden. Serve hot.

Note—If you do not have toy-size loaf pans, make your own by shaping a double thickness of foil to 4x2½x1½ size.

Miniature Lemon-Sugar Loaves

One package makes three loaves. Each person breaks off his own roll-size serving

Bake at 375° for 30 minutes.
Makes 3 little loaves

½ cup sugar
5 teaspoons grated lemon rind
4 tablespoons (½ stick) butter or margarine, melted
1 package (8 ounces) refrigerated flaky biscuits

1 Mix sugar and lemon rind on wax paper or foil; place melted butter or margarine in a pie plate.
2 Separate the 12 biscuits; dip each into melted butter or margarine, then in sugar mixture to coat well. Stand 4 each into ungreased toy-size loaf pans. Place pans on a cooky sheet for easy handling, if you wish.
3 Bake in moderate oven (375°) 30 minutes, or until golden. Serve hot.

Note—If you do not have toy-size loaf pans, make your own by shaping a double thickness of foil to 4x2½x1½ size.

Cheese-Stuffed Rye Round

Excellent as an appetizer or snack

Bake at 350° for 20 minutes.

1 one-pound round loaf rye bread
1 package (4 ounces) shredded Cheddar cheese

1 Divide rye bread into quarters cutting almost to but not through bottom crust. Cut each quarter into slices, again cutting almost to but not through the crust.

2 Sprinkle cheese between each slice of bread. Wrap loaf tightly in foil.
3 Bake in moderate oven (350°) for 20 minutes, or until cheese is melted.

Ribbon Cheese Loaf

Zippy cheese bakes melty-golden between layers of buttery rolls. Come summer, it's a perfect partner for salads

Bake at 375° for 45 minutes.
Makes 1 loaf

2 packages (8 ounces each) refrigerated butterflake or gem-flake rolls
1 cup grated Cheddar cheese (4 ounces)
1 tablespoon melted butter or margarine
½ teaspoon dried parsley flakes

1 Separate the 12 rolls in each package, then split each into 3 rounds. (It's easier if you work with 8 rolls, or 24 rounds, enough for one layer of the loaf, at a time. Rounds may not all be evenly thick, but this will not affect the baking.)
2 Arrange the 24 rounds, overlapping slightly, in 3 rows in bottom of a greased loaf pan, 9x5x3. Sprinkle with half of the grated cheese. Top with a second layer of 24 rounds, then remaining cheese; cover with remaining 24 rounds.
3 Brush loaf with melted butter or margarine; sprinkle evenly with parsley flakes.
4 Bake in moderate oven (375°) 45 minutes, or until golden. Cut in slices; serve hot.

Herb Ring-A-Round

Ready-mixed salad herbs and nutmeg combine for the tantalizing seasoner

Bake at 375° for 20 minutes.
Makes 1 nine-inch round loaf

4 tablespoons (½ stick) butter or margarine
2 teaspoons mixed salad herbs
⅛ teaspoon nutmeg
2 packages (8 ounces each) refrigerated butter-flake or gem-flake rolls

1 Melt butter or margarine in a small saucepan; stir in herbs and nutmeg.
2 Separate the dough in each package into 12 rolls; dip, 1 at a time, in butter mixture to coat both sides. Stand on edge, working from outside toward center, in a single layer in a buttered 9-inch pie plate.

(continued)

3 Bake in moderate oven (375°) 20 minutes, or until golden. Break into serving-size pieces with 2 forks. Serve hot.

HERB RING-A-ROUND

Separate refrigerated rolls, give each a buttery herb coat, and stand in their baker. To make the prettiest loaf, work from outside to center.

Onion Kuchen

Creamy-rich onion topper bakes over biscuits for this late-breakfast or supper hot bread

Bake at 375° for 30 minutes.
Makes 8 servings

2 medium-size onions, peeled, sliced, and separated into rings
3 tablespoons butter or margarine
1 package (8 ounces) refrigerated home-style or buttermilk biscuits
1 egg
1 cup (8-ounce carton) dairy sour cream
½ teaspoon salt
1 teaspoon poppy seeds

1 Sauté onions slowly in butter or margarine just until soft in a medium-size frying pan.
2 Separate the 10 biscuits; place in a single layer in an ungreased 8-inch layer-cake pan, pressing together to cover bottom completely. (Or, if you want to remove loaf from pan for party serving, bake in an 8-inch spring-form pan.) Spoon onion mixture on top.
3 Beat egg slightly in a small bowl; blend in

sour cream and salt. Spoon over onion mixture; sprinkle with poppy seeds.
4 Bake in moderate oven (375°) 30 minutes, or until topping is set. Slice in wedges; serve warm.

Double Nut-Date Ring

Brown-sugar—nut syrup gives a homemade touch to popular date-bread mix

Bake at 350° for 40 minutes.
Makes one 8-inch ring

½ cup (1 stick) butter or margarine
½ cup firmly packed brown sugar
½ teaspoon vanilla
½ cup pecans, slivered
1 package (17 ounces) date-nut quick bread mix
Egg
Water

1 Melt butter or margarine in a small saucepan; remove from heat. Stir in brown sugar and vanilla.
2 Sprinkle pecans into a greased 7-cup ring mold; carefully pour brown-sugar syrup over pecans.
3 Prepare date-bread mix with egg and water, following label directions; spoon over pecan mixture in mold.
4 Bake in moderate oven (350°) 40 minutes, or until a wooden pick inserted near center comes out clean. Let stand 10 minutes in mold on a wire rack; invert onto a serving plate. Serve warm or cold.

Sesame Whirls

After roast comes from the oven, turn up the heat to bake these little dinner breads

Bake at 375° for 12 minutes.
Makes 16 rolls

2 tablespoons sesame seeds
4 tablespoons (½ stick) butter or margarine, melted
2 packages refrigerated swirl dinner rolls

1 Place sesame seeds in a small frying pan; heat very slowly, shaking pan constantly, until seeds are lightly toasted. Spoon seeds and melted butter or margarine, dividing evenly, into 16 medium-size muffin-pan cups.
2 Separate the 8 rolls in each package; press,

one at a time, into muffin-pan cups, then turn seed side up.
3 Bake in moderate oven (375°) 12 minutes, or until golden; remove from pans. Serve hot.

Deviled Ham and Cheese Pinwheels

Packaged buttermilk biscuits take the work out of these delicious morsels

Bake at 450° for 10 minutes.
Makes 16 pinwheels.

1 can (2¼ ounces) deviled ham
½ cup shredded Swiss cheese (2 ounces)
2 tablespoons butter or margarine, melted
1 teaspoon freeze-dried chives
2 packages (8 ounces each) refrigerated buttermilk biscuits

1 Combine ham, cheese, chives, and butter or margarine in a small bowl; reserve.
2 On a lightly floured board, place 4 biscuits in a horizontal row overlapping each halfway; place 4 more biscuits in a row below and overlapping first row. Continue with remaining biscuits to form an 8-inch square.
3 Roll out with lightly floured rolling pin into a 10x16-inch rectangle. Press together any open spaces between the biscuits.
4 Spread ham and cheese filling evenly over rolled-out dough.
5 Roll up, lengthwise, jelly-roll fashion, keeping roll 16 inches long. Cut into 1-inch pieces with scissors or sharp knife. Tuck end of roll underneath pinwheel and place on lightly buttered cookie sheet.
6 Bake in a hot oven (450°) for 10 minutes, or until the pinwheels are lightly browned. Serve while still warm, with butter.

Tantalize the family with **Onion Kuchen** which looks hard to make, but isn't; and looks tasty, and is!

Strawberry Puffins

Their delicate fruit flavor comes from a can of instant drink mix

Bake at 400° for 10 minutes.
Makes 3½ dozen small muffins

½ cup strawberry-flavor drink mix
¾ cup milk
1 egg
2 tablespoons vegetable oil
2 cups biscuit mix
10X (confectioners' powdered) sugar

1 Combine drink mix, milk, egg and oil in a small bowl; beat with fork until well blended.
2 Add all at once to biscuit mix in medium-size

(continued)

bowl; stir just until biscuit mix is completely moistened. (Batter will be soft.)

3 Spoon into greased tiny muffin-pan cups (about 1¾x¾ inches), filling each two-thirds full.

4 Bake in hot oven (400°) 10 minutes, or until delicately golden but not browned.

5 Remove from pans; sprinkle tops with 10X sugar, serve hot.

Bacon-Cheese Puffs

A cube of sharp Cheddar melts in the center of each tender muffin as it bakes

> Bake at 400° for 25 minutes.
> Makes 12 muffins.

2 cups biscuit mix
5 slices crisp bacon, crumbled
¾ cup milk
1 egg
12 cubes Cheddar cheese (4 ounces)

1 Combine biscuit mix and crumbled bacon in a medium-size bowl; add milk and egg. Stir just to mix.

2 Spoon half of batter into 12 greased medium-size muffin-pan cups. Press a cheese cube into each muffin cup. Evenly spoon remaining batter over cheese, covering cheese completely.

3 Bake in hot oven (400°) 25 minutes, or until golden. Serve hot.

Corn Pillows

Golden brown with a hickory-flavored cheese filling

> Bake at 425° for 12 minutes.
> Makes 24 little rolls

1 package (10 ounces) corn-bread mix
¾ cup sifted all-purpose flour
1 teaspoon salt
1 teaspoon baking powder
½ teaspoon barbecue spice
¾ cup dairy sour cream
1 egg, beaten
1 roll (6 ounces) hickory-flavor process cheese food

1 Mix corn-bread mix, flour, salt, baking powder and barbecue spice in a large bowl. Stir in sour cream and egg until mixture forms a stiff dough

that leaves side of bowl clean. Form into a ball; divide in half.

2 Roll out dough, half at a time, ¼ inch thick on a lightly floured pastry cloth or board; cut into rounds with a floured 3-inch cookie cutter.

3 Cut 12 quarter-inch-thick slices from cheese; cut each in half. (Chill remaining cheese for a snack or sandwich.) Place a cheese crescent on half of each circle of dough; fold dough over to cover cheese; press edges together with a fork to seal. Place on a lightly greased large cookie sheet.

4 Bake in hot oven (425°) 12 minutes, or until rolls are firm and golden. Remove from cookie sheet to wire racks. Serve warm.

Corn-Biscuit Puffs

Accompany roast beef with these quick-to-fix biscuits

> Bake at 400° for 15 minutes.
> Makes 2½ dozen

2 packages (9 ounces each) corn-muffin mix
2 cups biscuit mix
2 eggs
1½ cups milk

1 Grease 30 large muffin-pan cups lightly, or place foil baking cups in pans.

2 Combine corn-muffin and biscuit mixes in a large bowl; add eggs and milk all at once. Stir mixture until evenly moist, then beat ½ minute. (Batter may still be slightly lumpy.) Spoon into prepared muffin-pan cups.

3 Bake in hot oven (400°) 15 minutes, or until golden. Remove from muffin cups; cool slightly on wire racks. Serve warm.

Day-before Note: Bake rolls ahead, then reheat before partytime. Place rolls in a large brown paper bag; close bag; sprinkle bag with a few drops water. Heat in moderate oven (350°) 5 to 10 minutes.

Polka-Dot Raisin Log

Fun to look at, and good to eat—children will ask for more

> Bake at 350° for 30 minutes.
> Makes 1 loaf, 9x5x3

1½ cups biscuit mix
¼ cup firmly packed light brown sugar
1 teaspoon grated orange rind

2 eggs
¼ cup water
½ cup semisweet-chocolate pieces
¼ cup chopped pecans
¼ cup seedless raisins
½ cup 10X (confectioners' powdered)
   sugar
Few drops vanilla

1 Combine biscuit mix, brown sugar, and orange rind in a large bowl. Vigorously stir in eggs and water; fold in chocolate pieces, pecans, and raisins.
2 Spoon into a generously buttered 5-cup mold or loaf pan, 9x5x3; spread top even. (If you're using a loaf pan, baked loaf will fill pan only halfway.)
3 Bake in moderate oven (350°) 30 minutes, or until puffed and golden. Loosen around edge with a knife; invert onto a wire rack.
4 Combine 10X sugar, vanilla, and 2 teaspoons water in a cup; blend until smooth and easy to pour from a spoon. Drizzle over loaf, letting mixture drip down side. Let stand until glaze sets. Slice crosswise; serve warm or cold.

Mantilla Braid

A braided loaf with a bacon-cheese and pimiento-stuffed olive filling

Bake at 375° for 20 minutes.
Makes 8 servings.

1 package refrigerated crescent rolls
1 jar (about 5 ounces) bacon-cheese spread
16 pimiento-stuffed olives, halved
1 tablespoon cream
1 tablespoon sesame seeds

1 Unroll crescent-roll dough into two rectangles; place, with sides slightly overlapping, on a large cookie sheet. Set cookie sheet on a damp towel to prevent slipping, then roll dough to a rectangle, 14x8.
2 Spread cheese in a 2-inch-wide strip down center of dough; place halved olives over cheese.
3 Make cuts in dough, 1 inch apart, from outer edges almost to filling; fold strips, alternating from side to side, across filling at an angle. Brush braid with cream; sprinkle with sesame seeds.
4 Bake in moderate oven (375°) 20 minutes, or until golden. Cut into slices; serve hot.

Sage Dinner Braid

Biscuit dough is rolled into ropes, then stacked to make this inviting loaf

Bake at 375° for 1 hour.
Makes 1 large loaf

4 cups biscuit mix
1 teaspoon ground sage
½ cup (1 stick) butter or margarine
1⅓ cups milk
2 teaspoons grated onion
1 egg, slightly beaten

1 Combine biscuit mix and sage in a medium-size bowl; cut in butter or margarine until mixture is crumbly. Add milk and grated onion; prepare, following label directions for rolled biscuits.
2 Divide into 18 pieces; roll each into a rope, 12 inches long. Braid each 3 ropes, pinching at ends to hold in place.
3 Place 3 braids, side by side, on a cooky sheet, shaping ends to an oval. Top with 2 more ropes for middle layer; place remaining on top. Brush all over with beaten egg.
4 Bake in moderate oven (375°) 1 hour, or until golden. Serve warm.

SAGE DINNER BRAID

Start with 18 "ropes" of dough; braid by threes. Then stack them, pyramid style, with three braids on bottom, two in middle, and a single one on top.

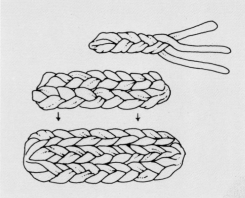

Rio Grande Corn Muffins

From start to finish, it only takes seventeen minutes to make these peppy muffins

Bake at 350° for 12 minutes.
Makes 6 muffins.

1 package (10 ounces) frozen corn muffins
½ cup shredded Muenster or Monterey Jack cheese (2 ounces)
1 or 2 green chili peppers (from a 4-ounce can)

1 Place frozen muffins on a cookie sheet. Divide cheese evenly on tops of muffins.
2 Remove seeds from peppers; cut into 12 strips. Place 2 strips crisscross on each muffin.
3 Bake in a moderate oven (350°) 12 minutes, or until lightly browned. Serve immediately.

Easy Cheese Boreks

These feathery, Turkish cheese-filled pastries are perfect to round out a soup and salad supper

Bake at 375° for 15 minutes.
Makes 16 boreks.

6 ounces cream cheese with chives, softened to room temperature
2 tablespoons grated Parmesan cheese
1 teaspoon Worcestershire sauce
2 to 3 drops liquid red-pepper seasoning
2 packages (8 ounces each) refrigerated crescent dinner rolls

1 Blend together cream cheese, Parmesan, Worcestershire and pepper-seasoning; reserve.
2 Unroll crescent rolls—do not separate at the perforations—then pat each of the 8 pieces to form a 4x6-inch rectangle. Cut each piece in half to form 2 squares. Spread 2 teaspoons of the cheese mixture over each piece of dough; roll, jelly-roll fashion.
3 Place boreks seam side down on an ungreased cookie sheet. Seal ends by crimping firmly with the tines of a fork. Bake, uncovered, in a moderate oven (375°), for about 15 minutes, or until the boreks are lightly browned.

Hot Herb Bread Sticks

Better double this recipe, for it's the kind of hot bread you just keep on eating

Bake at 400° about 5 minutes.
Makes 6 servings.

6 tablespoons butter or margarine
¼ cup chopped parsley
1 long thin loaf French bread
2 tablespoons grated Parmesan cheese

1 Cream butter or margarine in small bowl; stir in parsley.
2 Cut bread crosswise into thirds, then split each third in half to make 6 pieces; score cut sides about 1 inch apart almost through to crusts.
3 Spread tops and into cuts generously with butter-parsley mixture; sprinkle with cheese; place on cookie sheet.
4 Bake in hot oven (400°) about 5 minutes, or until golden-crisp.

Cheddar Cheese Twists

Start with refrigerated dinner rolls and you'll have these made in nothing flat

Bake at 375° for 12 minutes.
Makes 20 twists.

2 packages (8 ounces each) refrigerated Parker House dinner rolls
1½ cups shredded Cheddar cheese (6 ounces)
½ teaspoon leaf oregano
¼ teaspoon crushed red pepper

1 Separate rolls into individual rectangles.
2 Combine cheese, oregano and red pepper; blend well. Sprinkle evenly over each rectangle.
3 Grasp top right hand corner and bottom left hand corner of rectangle; twist in opposite directions and stretch to an 8-inch length. Place on buttered cookie sheet, pressing ends down slightly.
4 Bake in a moderate oven (375°) for 12 minutes, or until golden brown. Serve warm with butter.

INDEX